GOD'S REIGN
AND OUR UNITY

The Report of the Anglican-Reformed
International Commission 1981-1984

Woking, England, January 1984

SPCK   LONDON

THE SAINT ANDREW PRESS   EDINBURGH

First published in Great Britain 1984 by
SPCK
Holy Trinity Church
Marylebone Road
London NW1 4DU

and
The Saint Andrew Press
121 George Street
Edinburgh EH2 4YN

British Library Cataloguing in Publication Data

Anglican-Reformed International Commission
    God's reign and our unity.
    1. Christian union
    I. Title
    262'.72   BX8.2

ISBN 0-281-04129-6 (SPCK)
ISBN 0-7152-0578-1 (The Saint Andrew Press)

Typeset by Academic Typing & Typesetting Service
Gerrards Cross, Buckinghamshire SL9 8RZ
Printed in Great Britain by
Bocardo & Church Army Press Ltd, Cowley, Oxford

CONTENTS

ABBREVIATIONS

Abbreviations used in this Report include:

ACC	Anglican Consultative Council
ARCIC	Anglican–Roman Catholic International Commission
BEM	*Baptism, Eucharist and Ministry*
BWA	Baptist World Alliance
COCU	(US) Consultation on Church Union
WARC	World Alliance of Reformed Churches
WCC	World Council of Churches
CSI	Church of South India

PREFACE

This report is the result of work spread over four years (1981-4) by the Anglican–Reformed Commission which was set up after preliminary consultation in 1978. We were appointed by the Anglican Consultative Council and the World Alliance of Reformed Churches.

Those appointed to this Commission have greatly valued the growing and deepening fellowship which has developed during our meetings and we owe much in particular to the worship in daily prayer and Eucharist in which we have shared together and which remained the context in which we sought to do our work.

From the outset we sought to go behind the historical and traditional problems which have divided us since Reformation times and to put our quest for unity in new perspectives. We sought to do this by enquiring into the relationship between the Church and the Kingdom of God, the priority of grace, the trinitarian and christological basis of ministry, the mission of the Church.

We were fortunate in having in our membership representatives from Africa and Latin America and in being reminded by them that the divisions and differences that stemmed from the Reformation are not felt to be as important in many regions of the world as the divisions between rich and poor, black and white, men and women.

We were aware that our membership was not representative of Continental Europe or Asia, and was entirely male. Nevertheless we hope our findings will prove to be sensitive to the wide varieties of situations in which our member churches find themselves. A single report cannot, of course, do justice to every local situation but we hope groups will find in the report things to challenge them, and that they will also be aware of factors that are inadequately handled by us.

In submitting this report, we recommend that, in receiving and studying it, members of the Anglican and Reformed traditions will discuss this not only between themselves but where possible with other traditions too.

In our earlier meetings we were greatly helped by the Revd Dr John Huxtable who was the first co-chairman for the Reformed side and we regret that health reasons compelled him to resign from the Commission.

We should wish to thank also the Revd Richmond Smith, Theological Secretary for the World Alliance of Reformed Churches until 1983, who acted as co-secretary and who was succeeded by the Revd Dr Alan Sell for our final meeting.

We are indebted to our Anglican secretaries, the Revd David Chaplin who served us in the preliminary stage and the Revd George Braund who was with us throughout the four years of our Commission's life.

A special word of appreciation is due to Deirdre Hoban, Vanessa Wilde of London and Colette Jacot of Geneva who served our meetings so efficiently in the secretarial office.

CO-CHAIRMEN

John Tinsley	Roy F. Wilson
Bishop of Bristol	*United Church of Canada*
Anglican Consultative Council	World Alliance of Reformed Churches

January 1984, Woking, England

I OUR TASK

Origins of the Present Report

1   The World Alliance of Reformed Churches (WARC) represents 157 churches with about seventy million members. The Anglican Consultative Council (ACC) represents 27 provinces with about sixty-five million members. There are some parts of the world where only one of these two families of churches is represented. In Uganda and Tanzania, for example, there are large Anglican churches but no Reformed. In many countries of Europe, and in Indonesia, there are strong Reformed churches but few, if any, Anglicans. But there are large parts of the world where the two live side by side. Their distinctive and divergent styles of life and witness were developed during the struggles of the Reformation in Europe, and reflect the circumstances of that time and place. Now, four centuries later, they have become world communions. Both are committed to the ecumenical movement and have taken a leading part in it. Both have long been involved in discussions with each other and with other churches, in negotiations for union and – in the Indian sub-continent – in the formation of united churches.

2   These facts, and especially the fact that certain Anglican and Reformed churches have been actually united and now form together large and growing churches covering the whole of the Indian sub-continent, place our two communions in a relationship with each other which implies an obligation to press towards fuller unity. Both communions had their origin as distinct entities in the events of the Reformation, but both

confess themselves part of the one catholic Church, even though there are important differences between them in the ways they understand their continuity with the pre-Reformation Western Church. We are agreed that the unity we seek must be that of all Christian people, and it follows that 'the test of all local schemes of union is that they should express locally the principle of the great catholic unity of the Body of Christ' (Church of South India, Basis of Union, para. 1). But since that ultimate aim cannot be achieved in one leap, it is proper to ask that churches should at all times be ready to look for opportunities for small advances towards it. We believe that our two communions, within the wider fellowship of the universal Church, are well placed to take such steps in the many parts of the world where our member churches live side by side. We offer this Report in the hope that it will serve to encourage and guide such steps.

3   During the last 60 years Anglican and Reformed churchmen have taken a full part in multilateral discussions of the matters of faith and order which divide them, and have shared in the production of the recently published joint statement on 'Baptism, Eucharist and Ministry' (1982). Both have also been involved in bilateral conversations. The WARC has had such conversations with Lutherans, Baptists and Roman Catholics, and is exploring the possibility of dialogue with the Orthodox, Mennonites, Methodists and Churches of Christ (Disciples). Anglicans have had extensive dialogue with Lutherans, Old Catholics, Orthodox and Roman Catholics – the last of these having produced its 'Final Report' in 1982. A list of the major publications arising from these conversations is given in Appendix 1.

4   In spite of all this activity, and in spite of the

achievement of full organic union in North and South India, Pakistan and Bangladesh, recent years have seen a series of failures and disappointments in the quest for unity between our two communions. Plans for organic union between Anglican and Reformed churches which at one time seemed very promising have collapsed in Nigeria, Ghana, Sri Lanka, the Sudan, Canada, Australia and New Zealand. The United States Consultation on Church Union (COCU) has been at work for more than twenty years and has been obliged to move from the search for full organic union to exploring the idea of a covenant as a first stage, but progress towards this intermediate goal is uncertain. Proposals for covenanting in England and New Zealand have failed, and those in South Africa have suffered a serious setback. Committed as our two communions are to the quest for visible unity, we are bound to feel disappointed by this record of failure.

5 Accordingly the WARC and the ACC decided to call the first international consultation between the two bodies. A preliminary meeting was held in 1978, and subsequently four residential meetings of five to seven days each were held from 1981 to 1984. All of these meetings took place at St Columba's House, Woking, England. Throughout the meetings the members were able to share together in eucharistic worship and in morning and evening prayer according to the several traditions of our two communions. This shared worship has been of fundamental importance for the work of the commission. It is only as we meet in adoration of our one Lord that our minds are drawn into unison. It is necessary to make this point clear at the outset since, in our view, the fruitfulness of the Report will depend in large measure on the extent to which its examination

and reception in the member churches takes place within the same ambience of worship.

What keeps Anglicans and Reformed Apart?

6   Anglican and Reformed churches have found it possible to come together in united churches and to develop a common life in which both traditions could continue to play a part. Although representative theologians of both communions have been able to agree on the terms for proposed unions covering the matters of faith and order which have divided us, nevertheless, as we have seen, in most of the world these verbal agreements have not been enough to create unity. Is it possible to identify the factors which are still, apparently, stronger than the theological agreements which have been reached in some places? No doubt these factors are as varied as human nature itself, but some which are common to many situations can be listed even though they may apply in very different degrees in the many different places where our churches live and work. There are, of course, many controversies which occur within both our communions as well as between them. Some of these arise from the diversities of insight which will always characterize the life of the Church. Others need to be resolved within both our communions. We wish in this Report, however, to look at things which divide our two communions from one another. Some of these are specific to our two communions; others are things which apply generally to the life of churches.

Specific Obstacles

7   (*a*) Our two communions define themselves in different ways, and this makes mutual understanding difficult. Many churches within the Reformed tradition

have defined themselves in terms of subscription to a written confession, while those of the Congregational faith and order (many of whom are represented in the WARC), though never reluctant to devise declarations of the faith commonly held among them, have not made confessional subscription into a test of church membership. Anglicans have rather found their identity in a common liturgy and a common adherence to the threefold ministry. The Thirty-Nine Articles of the Church of England do not figure as largely in the self-understanding of Anglicans as the Book of Common Prayer does. In modern times Reformed churches have devoted much time and effort to the preparation of confessional documents restating the faith in con-temporary terms, or else (as at Barmen in 1934 and at Ottawa in 1982) declaring heretical certain doctrines or practices. Anglican churches, meanwhile, have laboured to revise their forms of worship in the light of changing situations. Much might be written about the relative importance of these two exercises, and there is much need on each side to reflect on the value of the other. The fact remains, however, that this difference is expressive of a deep divergence of the ways in which the two churches understand themselves, and a correspond-ingly serious difficulty in understanding the other. The difference separates what belongs together. The danger here is of a kind of 'nominalism' – the confusing of form and substance. We have tended, in scholastic fashion, to identify too absolutely our formulations of the truth with the truth as it is in Jesus, and our forms of worship as the definitive ways of participating in him. We have thus judged one another by our outward forms. When the late Pope John XXIII had the courage to say that the substance of ancient doctrine is one thing but our formulations are another, he opened the door for reformation and the reformulation of doctrine, and so for the renewal sought in Vatican II. It was a plea for a 'realist' understanding which broke with Tridentine 'nominalism' and dogmatism. So, as Anglicans and Reformed, we must look together beyond our rigid formulations of doctrine and forms of worship to the reality of what we are in Christ, so that we may find formulations of doctrine and forms of worship which truly bear witness to the gospel of grace. The Church is *semper reformanda* in the light of Christ and the gospel. We must learn to accept one another for what we are in God's grace, and not simply judge one another by our outward forms, important as these are.

8 (*b*) Both our communions affirm the centrality of word and sacrament in the life of the Church, but the accent falls differently. At their best Anglicans honour the faithful preaching of the word and Reformed have a deep reverence for the sacraments. But it cannot be denied that we habitually fall short of our best, and because we fail in different ways we are very conscious of the failures of the other. Reformed churchmen can point to the meagre quality of some Anglican preaching, and Anglicans can point to the shallowness of some eucharistic practice in Reformed churches.

9 (*c*) The role of the bishop in Anglican piety and churchmanship has no exact parallel in Reformed experience. We are not speaking here of the strictly ecclesiological and theological factors involved in the difference between Anglican and Reformed patterns of oversight. Even when these are reconciled, there remains as a point of real difference the importance given to the bishop as the one who, in a more than functional sense, stands as a personal symbol of the catholicity and apostolicity of the Church. Reformed churchmanship

has not developed anything exactly comparable to this, and perhaps it is at this point that one of the deepest emotional barriers to union lies.

10 (*d*) The tradition of the Anglican churches was initially shaped in the sixteenth century by the Elizabethan settlement, and in the seventeenth century by the antagonism created by the Civil War and the Restoration. The world-wide development of the Anglican communion in the eighteenth and nineteenth centuries was intimately connected with the expansion of British imperial power. The fact that the Church of England has thus such intimate relations with the state, and that until recently the Anglican churches in many parts of the world were seen as closely related to the colonial power, has strongly affected relations with other churches. The Reformed churches have had in the past, and still have in Scotland and in some parts of Europe, a comparable (though not identical) bond of union with the state. In the British Isles these close bonds between church and state are still important obstacles to full mutual acceptance, and their consequences in other parts of the world are not irrelevant.

11 (*e*) More subtle, but not less important, are the bonds which tie our two communions to the national feeling and the folk religion of the people to whom we minister. The feeling, in England, for example, that the Anglican form of worship and church order is 'the religion of the English people', and in Scotland that the Presbyterian forms similarly embody the proper religion of the Scots is often deep and enduring. English and Scots people who have migrated to other parts of the world have carried these sentiments with them, and they have lost none of their strength on the journey. In North America the different denominational forms tend

to be seen as optional varieties of one common religion which is proper to the nation as a whole. In some parts of the Third World, through the accidents of missionary history, membership in an Anglican or a Reformed church is intimately related to membership in a particular tribal or ethnic group, and – in such places – the church can be defined as the church of that people more appropriately than as the church of a confession.

General Obstacles

12 (a) There are obstacles to unity which operate in all encounters between churches and are not confined to the Anglican-Reformed dialogue; they need, however, to be recognized. One of the most important of these is the fear that union means loss of identity. This fear goes very deep. No one becomes a Christian, and no one grows up into mature Christian discipleship except through forms of teaching, worship, practice and piety which have been developed in a particular tradition. Apart from an encounter with Christians nurtured in another tradition, there is no occasion for making a distinction between the substance and the form – between the presence of Christ himself and the forms in which he has made himself present to the disciple. In this sense there is a 'natural fundamentalism' in regard to the forms of churchmanship which is quite proper. When the encounter takes place with a Christian nurtured in another tradition, there arises the painful necessity of going beyond and behind the received form to a new apprehension of the substance – of the presence of Christ himself. This is a kind of fresh conversion. It cannot be easy. It should not surprise us that it is resisted with passionate intensity, because resistance seems to be required by fidelity to Christ as he has made himself known to us in the past. As with all true con-

version, this can only be the work of the Holy Spirit, for which we have to pray.

13 (b) A further difficulty which besets all moves towards organic union is the widespread and well-grounded fear of large organizations. In spite of many disclaimers, it is widely feared that organic unity will lead to the uniformity which frequently seems to be the inevitable – even if unintended – consequence of large-scale organization. While we cannot admit a dichotomy between 'visible unity' and 'spiritual unity', we must both insist that a deep spiritual unity in Christ is the necessary precondition of unity of structure, and also devote more effort to the adumbration of structures designed to ensure that 'visible unity' does not mean bureaucratically controlled uniformity.

14 (c) Among the most pervasive and powerful of all the factors which combine to paralyse the movement towards unity is a false understanding of the nature of the Church and of God's calling to the Church. For too many Christians the Church is seen only in static terms, the religious aspect of society, a home of refuge from the storms of life, a bark to carry the passengers safe into harbour – or rather a flotilla of boats among which each person is free to choose the most attractive. So long as the Church is seen in this way there will be no urgency about the quest for unity. Our Report is written in the conviction that the Church is to be understood in a much more dynamic way, as a pilgrim people called to a journey whose goal is nothing less than God's blessed Kingdom embracing all nations and all creation, a sign, instrument and foretaste of God's purpose 'to sum up all things with Christ as head' (Eph. 1.10). It is only in this missionary and

eschatological[1] perspective that the question of unity is rightly seen.

Christian Unity and Human Unity

15   From this perspective it is possible to look in a new way at the disappointments and obstacles to which we have referred in the previous section. In the course of our Report we shall suggest ways in which some of these difficulties may be met, but at the outset we must confess that many of these arise because of a wrong understanding of the nature and calling of the Church. When the Church is understood as an end in itself and not as a sign and foretaste of the Kingdom, then the quest for ecclesiastical unity is seen as irrelevant to the great issues of God's rule of justice and peace. For, as has to be sadly confessed, the Church itself has often been guilty of complicity in and perpetration of all kinds of injustices to those who – for whatever reason – are pushed to the margins of society. It has sometimes condoned and even called down God's blessing on violence. Too often its theological statements have pretended to a universal truth above all party conflict, but in fact they have reflected the interests of those who wielded power. They have been ideologically tainted.

16   In this situation, it is often said, discussions about the respective merits of bishops and presbyteries are an irrelevance. The unification of these corrupted churches would make matters not better but worse. The real divisions are not the traditional ones of faith and order, but the divisions on issues of justice and peace. The

---

[1]   Eschatology is that part of Christian doctrine which concerns the last things – the coming again of Christ, judgement, the kingdom of God and eternal life.

first need, therefore, is that the churches themselves should be liberated from captivity to the interests of the powerful in order to become instruments of liberation for others.

17   These often passionate affirmations must serve to call us back from a false view of the Church to one which is dynamic and missionary. This will mean that our quest for Christian unity is seen steadily in the context of God's purpose to reconcile all people and all things in Christ. According to the Fourth Gospel Jesus said: 'I, when I am lifted up will draw all men to myself' (John 12.32). The Church is called to be the first-fruits and sign of that promise which is for all mankind. Its disunity is a sin against that promise. Church unity would be a false unity if it were not for the sake of the fulfilling of that promise in all its universal scope. The 'Faith and Order' movement was born in the context of a missionary concern. The pioneers of the movement drew their inspiration and their guidance from the prayer of Jesus that his disciples might be one 'so that the world may believe' (John 17.21). They sought unity not as an end in itself but for the sake of mission. Yet it must be acknowledged that this perspective has sometimes been lost. It needs to be reaffirmed that if we seek for unity among Christians it can only be in order that the Church may become a more credible sign, instrument and foretaste of God's purpose to 'unite all things with Christ as head' (Col. 1.19f., cf. Eph. 1.10).

18   If it is wrong to separate the question of church unity from the question of the unity of humankind, it is also wrong and delusive to propose 'justice' and 'peace' as goals to be sought apart from a shared life in

Christ. If 'justice' is conceived as an abstract principle, the pursuit of it is a recipe for endless war, because all human beings overestimate what is due to themselves and underestimate what is due to others. Belligerents invariably claim to be fighting for justice. The Christian faith is that God's justice has been made manifest and available in the actual event of Christ's atonement, and that it is here at the cross that it can be received as a gift by faith and become the basis for actual justice among human beings. So also 'peace' pursued as an abstract concept can only delude us. The most devastating wars are fought among the promoters of rival programmes for peace. The Christian faith is that God has made peace through Jesus 'by the blood of his cross' (Col. 1.20), so establishing the one valid centre for the unity of the whole human family. But these statements are mere words unless they are embodied (even if only provisionally) in a visible community in which the righteousness of God and the peace of God are actually known and experienced in reality – even though it is only a foretaste of the full reality. The Church is not authorized or empowered to represent a justice and a peace other than the justice and peace offered to the world in the atoning work of Christ. But it contradicts its own nature and calling when its members are unable to live together in a reconciled fellowship. Concern for the unity of all humankind is the only proper context for the quest of church unity; it is not a reason for abandoning that quest.

A Wider Perspective

19 It may help the reader of this Report to understand its main thrust if we record how we came to put together our dual concern for the unity of the

Church and for the unity of humanity. The initial approach of our European and North American members was to look again at the theological and sociological factors which have kept our Churches apart (see, for example, paras. 6-14 above). Such topics as 'Establishment' in England and 'Subscription to Confessions' in the Reformed Churches of Great Britain, have too often been examined politically and ecclesiastically rather than theologically and pastorally. This has impeded ecumenical advance, the phrase 'National Church' being so differently understood in diverse denominational settings.

20   The Commission was made very conscious of the need to distinguish the purely cultural and political factors in the traditions of separated Anglican and Reformed Churches. The disentangling of some of these factors gave a new reality to the Commission's task, helping us to focus more clearly on the biblical and theological basis for the exchange of views, and so to follow a properly theological line in the faith and order discussion.

21   These theological and sociological factors had their sources in Europe and North America; but it was disturbing to recognize just how many of the ecclesiastical, political, social and national tensions and misunderstandings, which affect relationships among our member churches in the United Kingdom churches, had been exported to territories of the British Commonwealth and elsewhere, affecting indigenous churches, both Anglican and Reformed, in such areas. These inherited prejudices and divisions still cause perplexity and leave traces of strain and antagonism in many Third World churches.

22   The initial approach of those coming from Anglican and Reformed churches in the Third World, to serve on this small international group, was to stress the seeming irrelevance of many traditional discussions on Christian unity and Church reunion in the face of the desperate social problems facing their countries. From South Africa we were warned of new and perhaps graver threats to the unity of the Churches based on racial discrimination, and from Latin America we were made aware of the divisions between Christians, some supporting oppressive systems and others opting for the struggle to end them. The North Americans warned of sexual discrimination in the Church. The plea of our members from the Third World was to make 'ortho-praxis' the significant issue between divided Churches, notably the position taken by individual Churches on the issue of apartheid in Southern Africa. Agreement on Christian principles and practice was presented as the first priority in bringing Churches together. A response to this Third World sense of urgency over 'orthopraxis' in a threatened world introduced a salutary note of realism into the discussions, and led the participants to take a fresh look at priorities in the ecumenical movement.

23   All this meant a new emphasis on the unity of the human race as the goal of the Christian gospel, with the Kingdom of God restored as a focus for ecclesiology. The Commission proceeded with its task with a world-related feeling of urgency, seeing its theological task to be not so much academic as essentially evangelical. The faith and order task was then taken up in terms of the final goal of the Kingdom. This numerically small Anglican-Reformed International Commission worked in this freshly discovered world-wide context and within the ultimate dimension of the Kingdom of God – that is

to say, the reign of God in which creation and human community are renewed by the Spirit through their transformation in Christ.

24   This concern for the unity of humanity in the purpose of God provided the antidote to the self-centredness referred to in paragraph 14 above. We realized that the most effective way of overcoming the apathy which is threatening the ecumenical movement is to put much more closely together concern for the unity of the Church and for the unity of humanity in the purpose of God. The rest of our Report attempts to do this.

II THE CHURCH:
GOD'S APOSTOLIC PEOPLE

Debtors to Grace

25   In spite of all the factors which continue to keep
our two traditions apart, we join with the whole Christian
family in confessing one, holy, catholic and apostolic
Church. The goal of church unity is the reconciliation of
humanity and the whole universe to God, and the
source and impetus for that unity are to be found in
God himself; for the Gospels testify to the unity between
Jesus Christ and the Father (John 10.30; Matt. 11.27),
and between the Father and the Spirit (John 15.26),
and Jesus prays that his disciples may be drawn into
that unity (John 17.21). The pattern of unity in diversity is thus in the Godhead. The God whose being is
holy love, uniting the Father, Son and Spirit, draws us
by the work of the Spirit into participation in the Son's
love and obedience to the Father. This same holy love
draws us to one another. This is grace, and to reject
one another is to reject God's grace. The reason why we
can never rest content in our separation is the unlimited
grace of God the Father, who has accepted us in the
beloved Son and bound us together in his own life by
the power of the Holy Spirit – a life in which we are
called to reflect both the unity and diversity of the
Godhead. If then we refuse to accept one another
in Christ we flout the grace by which he has accepted
us and by which we live.

26   God by this sheer grace has called a people to be
bound to him in total fidelity. The Old Testament
portrays the Lord as the lover who for ever seeks the

faithfulness of his own bride. The New Testament bears witness to the decisive events in which the Father sent forth his own beloved Son to take upon himself and redeem our sin-stained humanity, and anointed him by the Spirit to do the mighty works which manifest his kingly presence. The climax of these mighty works was the victorious passion in which the ruler of this world was cast down from his seat of power. With that victory accomplished, Jesus sent forth his disciples, empowered by the Spirit, to continue that which he had been sent by the Father to do (John 20.19-23). This purpose of the Father is nothing less than 'to reconcile all things to himself, whether on earth or in heaven' in Christ who is both the head of the whole cosmos and also the head of that body which is sent into the world as the first-fruits of his reconciling work (Col. 1.15-23). As those who have been 'reconciled in his body of flesh by his death' (v.22) they are to 'hold fast to the head', from whom the whole body, nourished and knit together through its joints and ligaments grows with a growth that is from God' (Col. 2.19). They thus belong already to the new creation in which all the natural barriers that hold human beings apart are transcended (Col. 3.11).

27 All of our life in Christ - as Paul never tires of insisting - is based on 'the immeasurable riches of (God's) kindness towards us in Christ Jesus' (Eph. 2.7). This kindness is despised and flouted when we fail to live together in that unity which his unconditional kindness both enables and requires. We are summoned to accept one another as freely as God in Christ has accepted us (Rom. 15.7). If we have been 'reconciled to God in one body through the cross' (Eph. 2.16), then to break into fractions is to commit the enormity of dis-membering the body of our Saviour (1 Cor. 1.13). The

life which we share in Christ is both deeply personal and inescapably corporate. The love of God poured into our hearts by the Spirit binds us at the same time to our brothers and sisters. This love is continually renewed through an interior commitment in love and obedience to the Saviour. This is something profoundly personal. But it expresses itself in a commitment of love and obedience to the other ('Be servants one of another') which issues in the life of a visible human community. Hence it is that in that prayer in which Jesus consecrated himself as an offering to the Father, and in the same act consecrated his disciples to be offered in him, he also prayed that they might be kept in the same unity which binds him to the Father. Their corporate life is to be nothing less than a real participation in the life of the triune God – a life lived always in Christ and offered to the Father through the power of the Spirit. When it is so, there will be a credible witness to the world of God's action in Christ (John 17.21).

28   The prayer of Jesus from which these words are taken, acknowledges, as does the whole Gospel, the darkness in which the light shines. The gospel of God's grace can be rejected and seen not as good news but as threat. People may choose darkness rather than light, and the Church, which is sent not to judge but to bring the word of salvation, can become the occasion for conflict and rejection. Christ, who is the rock on whom we build, is the stone of stumbling for those who reject his invitation to enter the new age and become children who live only by grace. We are warned at many points in Scripture that judgement begins with the house of God and not all who say 'Lord, Lord' will be acknowledged by the Lord at the end as his. We are not permitted to prescribe limits to unity or to pretend that there are

none. This does not lessen but heightens the urgency of the quest for unity. We are sent to call all people to the faith and obedience of Christ and we must trust him to gather his own at the end.

First-Fruits of a New Creation

29   It is essential to approach the question of unity among Christians in this missionary and eschatological context. The Church is sent into the world as sign, instrument and first-fruits of a reality which comes from beyond history – the Kingdom, or reign of God. The unity of the Church is not simply an end in itself because the Church does not exist for itself but for the glory of God and as a sign, instrument and first-fruits of his purpose to reconcile all things in heaven and earth through Christ. Nor is the unity of the Church merely a means to an end, for the Church already enjoys a foretaste of that end, and is only a sign and instrument in so far as it is a foretaste. Life in Christ is the end for which all things were made, not a means to an end beyond it.

30   The Church is thus a provisional embodiment of God's final purpose for all human beings and for all creation. It is an embodiment because it is a body of actual men and women chosen by God to share through the Spirit in the life of Christ and so in his ministry in the world. It is provisional in a double sense: only part of the human family has been brought into its life, and those who have been so brought are only partly conformed to God's purpose. If they were fully conformed they would be fully reconciled to one another. The quest for unity is one aspect of the Church's acting out of her unceasing prayer: 'Your kingdom come.'

By holding steadily in view both the corporeality of the Church, its embodiment of Christ's life in the life of an actual community, and its provisionality in relation to the Kingdom, we are able to expose the fallacies underlying the three following arguments which are often directed against the quest for visible unity.

31 (*a*) Some affirm that concern for unity deflects attention from the more urgent business of evangelism, and they (correctly) point out that groups less interested in unity are often among the most successful in achieving numerical growth. To this it must be replied that if the Church were an end in itself then it would follow that multiplication of numbers would be the criterion by which priorities should be judged, but if the Church is a sign and first-fruits of the reconciliation of all things in Christ, the fruit of evangelism should be communities reconciled to one another in Christ. If men and women are not being drawn into the one body, we must ask whether in fact their growth in Christ is not being stunted. 'Rather, speaking the truth in love, we are to grow up in every way into him who is the head, into Christ, from whom the whole body, joined and knit together by every joint with which it is supplied, when each part is working properly, makes bodily growth and upbuilds itself in love' (Eph. 4.15–16). The mere multiplication of cells, unrelated to the purpose of the body, is a sign not of life and health, but of cancer and death.

32 (*b*) Others declare that issues of justice and peace are more important from the viewpoint of the Kingdom than the ecclesiastical issues of faith and order. To this it must be replied that if the Church were merely a means to an end, then it would have to be judged by

its effectiveness in promoting a more just and free social order. But even the best social order is not the final goal of human existence. Christians have sometimes forgotten that the Church, while it is only a provisional embodiment of the new creation, is nevertheless a real embodiment enjoying by God's grace a real foretaste here and now of the righteousness and peace and joy of journey's end. When this is forgotten, Christianity is turned into a mere ideological crusade, and its actions for justice and peace are robbed of their essential and distinctive character – namely the presence here and now of the peace and righteousness of God given freely to sinful men and women. The Church is a sign and the first-fruits of the ultimate order which transcends history. In so far as it is a true sign and the true first-fruits, it will also have an instrumental value in promoting justice and freedom in the transient social order of history, but in so far as it contradicts in its own life the order which it is called to signify and (provisionally) embody, it fails in the one task which is entrusted to it.

33   (c) Still others say that unity must not be pursued at the expense of truth. This is right. But if the Church is a sign and the first-fruits of God's purpose to reconcile all things in Christ, then all formulations of truth must be judged by their relation to the central reality of God's redeeming and reconciling work in Christ. Doctrines which deny or devalue this must – in the name of faithfulness – be resisted. Nevertheless it is not required that all doctrinal matters must be agreed before unity is possible. That would be to deny the provisionality of the Church in relation to the Kingdom. In fact it frequently happens that, when matters of doctrine and practice are held to justify continued separation, the supreme truth, which is Christ himself, is publicly denied

in the name of lesser truths which are held in separation. We are more likely to reach unanimity as a result of accepting one another in Christ and then working out our differences in one fellowship than by giving them in effect a status higher than that of the one supreme truth given to us in Christ. The experience of churches which have taken the risk of union even when there had been wide disagreement abundantly confirms this.

34   Too often the concern for evangelism, social justice and church unity are set against each other, different groups demanding that primary or exclusive attention be given to one or another of these concerns. The Father, however, sent his Son to preach the gospel, to proclaim justice for the oppressed and to draw together all his disciples into the unity of the Godhead. He has enlisted us to participate in his work through the power of the Spirit. He gives gifts so that all his disciples may perform their distinctive work as different members of his one body. Evangelism, social justice and church unity are not conflicting concerns, but are complementary aspects of the one mission of God in which we participate as accountable stewards. To restrict our concern to any one of them would be to abridge the gospel.

Sent to All the Nations

35   As a provisional embodiment of God's purpose of reconciliation, the Church must understand itself as a people in pilgrimage, accepting with gratitude the resting places given on the way, but always ready to move when it is clear that faithfulness to the one calling of the one Lord requires it, an Abrahamic community, ready to live in tents, looking always to the

city whose builder and maker is God (Heb. 11.10). The decisions required with regard to the reunion of our separated communions have to be made in the context of pilgrimage towards a goal which no one has yet reached. This pilgrimage is a missionary pilgrimage. The Church is apostolic both in tracing its origin through the first apostles and in continuing that apostolate today. The Church's journey is both to the ends of the earth and to the end of the age. The disciples were called by Jesus to be with him and to be sent in the power of the Spirit. In the same way the Church abides in Christ through the Spirit only as it goes with him on the mission entrusted to him by the Father.

36 This missionary perspective is being rediscovered in contemporary teaching about the Church. (Consider the opening words of the Second Vatican Council's 'Constitution on the Church': 'Christ is the light of the Nations'.) This rediscovery was necessary because the ecclesiastical forms which developed at the time of the Reformation (our own included) were shaped by the 'Christendom' perspective of that time. Although the great reformers were seeking to return to Scripture and the Fathers to find models on which reformation could be based, their thinking was inevitably shaped by the society in which they lived, a society understood as Christian in which all (except Jews) were baptized, in which church and society were effectively coterminous, and which had no regular contact with the world of the non-Christian religions – apart from the military encounter with Islam as the enemy on the frontiers of Christendom. Consequently our theologies and ecclesiologies have been developed in dialogue (often polemical) between different versions of churchmanship rather than in missionary encounter with the unevangelized

world. The rediscovery of a missionary perspective has been made possible by the experience of the world-wide Church during the recent centuries of missionary expansion. This has helped us to enter again into the perspective of the New Testament, where the Church is a small evangelizing community in a pagan society, ministry is primarily leadership in mission, baptism is commitment to that mission, and Eucharist is the continual renewal of that commitment.

37   This missionary context provides new perspectives for the controversies about ministry, word and sacrament which have traditionally divided our two communions. We hope that our present report illustrates the validity of these new perspectives as we come to deal with these matters. It is important to hold this missionary perspective in close relation to what has been said about the provisionality of the Church in relation to the Kingdom. It has been said that there are two aspects of this provisionality; only *part* of the human family has been enlisted for Christ, and those who have been enlisted show only a very *partial* obedience. These two aspects are mutually related. As the Church goes out to bear witness to Christ among the nations, its own partial understanding of God's purpose is corrected and enlarged.

38   This is because mission is not simply the action of the Church enlarging its own borders. Mission is the sovereign action of the Holy Spirit who, through the faithful words and deeds of the Church, bears witness to Jesus (John 15.26) and does his own work of convicting the world (John 16.8–11) and of leading the Church into a fuller understanding of the Father's will (John 16.12–15). As in the Old Testament, so also in the New, the work of gathering all the nations to become God's

people and to worship him from whom their life comes, is the work of God himself. It is the presence of the Spirit, foretaste of the eschatological Kingdom, which constitutes the effective witness to Jesus. The human occasions for the Spirit's work include both words and deeds, all springing from and expressing the life of the one body which lives for the praise and adoration of God. Where there is a shared life centred in the worship and service of God the Father, rooted in Christ as he is made known to us in Scripture, interpreted in the teaching of faithful witnesses all down the ages, and sustaining the free exercise of the Spirit's varied gifts of speech and action among all the members, there the sovereign Lord, the Spirit, both gathers the peoples and leads the Church into fuller understanding. It is within this missionary perspective that we can begin to overcome the partial understandings which have kept our two communions apart.

III LIFE IN THE CHURCH

Orthodoxy and Orthopraxis

39   The Church owes its being to that which has been done once for all in the incarnation, ministry, passion, resurrection and ascension of the Lord Jesus Christ whom we acknowledge and confess as the Son, the second person of the triune God. The Church lives only in dependence upon him, the Head, and this dependence consists in faith, love and obedience. It has therefore been at all times the necessary concern of the Church that faith, love and obedience should be directed exclusively to their true object. The Church has sought, and must always seek, both in its worship and in its teaching, to find words which are faithful to the Church's Lord. Orthodoxy means both true teaching and true worship. As we have noted above (Para. 7), Reformed Churches have tended to emphasize the former and Anglicans the latter, but we agree that both are essential and that in this respect each of our communions can learn from the other.

40   Orthodoxy is not maintained simply by repeating the same words. In its missionary advance the Church is always required to find in the languages of those who are brought to faith from many cultures, words which direct their minds in teaching and worship to the one true God. Likewise, as the Church continues to hand on the faith in each new age, it is required to find new words which, in the language of these new generations, will rightly express that faith. Both our communions, receiving the Scriptures as the authoritative standard of faith, acknowledge the need for this continuing effort of reformulation both in teaching and in worship.

41   Although our predecessors took different paths at the time of the Reformation, they had a common concern to restore 'the face of the ancient Catholic Church' (Calvin), through a return to Scripture and the Fathers. Today both our communions acknowledge our dependence on the credal and liturgical formulations of the earliest centuries. Both recognize our need to remain open to the witness of Christians of other traditions and - since we contain within our membership people of many different cultures - to learn from Christians of all continents and of all races, so that our contemporary teaching and worship may truly express the fullness of God's purpose to reconcile all humankind in Christ. All of this is implicit in our commitment to the ecumenical movement.

42   Within this movement new contacts with the Orthodox churches have placed some of the inter-confessional conflicts of the Western churches in fresh perspective. They have stimulated thought on the doctrine of the Trinity and its centrality by reopening discussion of the *filioque* clause[2] in the Western version of the Nicene Creed. Though this doctrine of the Trinity, fundamental to our faith, has never been denied in either the Anglican or Reformed tradition, yet we confess that it has not occupied the central place which belongs to it and which it has held among the Orthodox. The image of God in the minds of many people in our churches is a unitary one - the solitary creator, the prime mover of the philosophers. Consequently the doctrine

---

[2]   In the original form of the Nicene creed, still used in the Eastern Orthodox churches, it is said that the Spirit proceeds from the Father. The Western churches subsequently added the words 'and from the Son' (Latin *filioque*). This addition, made without the agreement of a universal council, has been a cause of disagreement between the Eastern and Western churches ever since.

of the Trinity has been regarded as an incomprehensible mystification of something simple.

43   Nevertheless it lies at the very foundation of our life in Christ, as well as of the faith which sustains it, that God – the one and only God – is Father, Son and Spirit in the perfect unity of love; that the divine being is therefore not solitary but always and from eternity a being in love; and that in our life in Christ we are made participants in this being-in-love - as Christ prayed for believers that they might be made one in the unity which he has with the Father (John 17.21). Just as we believe that man has been created by God to have his being-in-love, so in the Church we participate in the life of the triune God in fulfilment of the purpose of creation. This must govern decisively our life in the Church and our concern for the world.

44   Orthodoxy, which is both right believing and right worshipping – that is to say, belief and worship directed to the truth, the reality of the triune God – cannot be severed from right practice. Faith and love belong together with obedience. 'If you keep my commandments', said Jesus, 'you abide in my love.' The Church is under obligation to guard the true faith expressed, and constantly needing fresh expression, in teaching and worship. It must be able, when need arises, to warn against forms of teaching and worship which lead those who use them away from the true God, and if necessary to draw a line of demarcation at the point where falsehood threatens truth. But if faith, love and obedience belong inseparably together, it follows that the Church may have to take like action in respect of conduct which contradicts the truth by which the Church lives. The World Alliance of Reformed Churches has recently

acted - after years of unproductive discussion - to suspend from its membership churches which adhere to the ideology and practice of *apartheid*. The breach has occurred in this case not because of differences about the doctrines which have traditionally divided the churches, but because of adherence to a practice held to be incompatible with obedience to Christ. It is a matter of orthopraxis rather than of orthodoxy. There are many Christians who think that racial separation is not the only issue of praxis on which the Church may have to use the word 'heresy' and exercise the discipline of suspension from communion. The continued acquies-cence of churches in the monstrous injustices of the present international economic order may well be another such matter.

45   No discussion of Christian unity in the contem-porary world can escape this question. True believing (orthodoxy) should bear fruit in right action (ortho-praxis). Yet, because Christians are sinners, they fail to embody in their conduct what they profess in their creed. The Church is a fellowship in which Christ con-sents to eat and drink with sinners. But the Church is also called to be a school of holiness in which the members 'teach and admonish one another in all wis-dom' (Col. 3.16) in order that its members may be 'presented holy and blameless and irreproachable' before its Lord (Col. 1.22). Conduct contradictory of our faith which refuses correction and which, as in both the examples we are considering, entrenches itself in a false theology or ideology, cannot indefinitely be held within the Christian fellowship.

46   We have to confess that our search for ecclesi-astical unity will be disobedience to the Church's Lord if it does not go hand in hand with the mutual

correction and admonition of which the Apostle speaks, and if it is not ready to face the painful possibility of excommunication where this correction is refused, or where the wrong practice is entrenched and defended within a doctrinal formulation which fails to acknowledge Christ as the sole Lord of both Church and world. Such a painful possibility must be recognized. So far as our two communions are concerned, the division – if it occurred – would not be between but within each of them.

Baptism

47   Baptism has not been an issue in dispute between our two traditions, yet our common practice of baptism has not led us into that unity which is stated by St Paul to be the necessary implicate of one baptism. According to him, all who are baptized into Christ constitute in him one body in which there cannot be divisions (Gal. 3.27f.; 1 Cor. 12.13; Eph. 4.4f.). We have to ask whether our failure to draw the proper conclusions from our common baptism is evidence of failure in both our communions to understand fully its meaning.

48   (a) According to all the four Gospels, the beginning of the public ministry of Jesus was his baptism by John in the River Jordan. The practice of Christian baptism in water, which we share with the universal Church, looks back to this decisive event, and it is here that we must begin to understand its meaning. John's message concerned the imminence of the day of the Lord. It was a call to repentance in view of threatened judgement. The baptism in water which John administered was a prophetic sign accompanying and enforcing the message. Jesus, the sinless one, went down into the waters of

Jordan in solidarity with our sinful race, submitting vicariously to the judgement of God upon guilty sinners. The coming judge was the man judged for sinners, the lamb of God who takes away the sin of the world. In that action Jesus was acknowledged by the Father as the beloved Son and anointed by the Spirit for his mission. This is the event which marks 'the beginning of the gospel' (Mark 1.1; cf. Acts 1.22; 10.37). The triune God has taken up into his own being the sinful history of the world. 'For our sake he made him to be sin who knew no sin, so that in him we might become the righteousness of God' (2 Cor. 5.21).

49   The baptism of Jesus looked towards its fulfilment in his total life and ministry. From his baptism Jesus is driven by the Spirit first into the desert to meet and master in single combat the power that opposes God's purpose, and then, having 'bound the strong man' (Mark 3.27), into the towns and villages of Galilee to release those who had been his captives. The baptism had to be implemented in this active engagement with the prince of this world, consummated on the cross where the 'ruler of this world' is cast out (John 12.31), and vindicated in the resurrection.

50   Jesus' baptism as the servant (cf. Isaiah 42.1ff.) is thus a baptism into death, and he speaks during his ministry of his coming death as his baptism (Luke 12.50, Mark 10.38). In the Marcan phrase just referred to, Jesus warns his disciples that they will be required to share this baptism into death, and in St Paul's writings we are likewise reminded that our baptism is into his death (Rom. 6.3), so that as we die with him we may also rise with him (Rom. 6.5). The 'one baptism', which following St Paul we confess in our creed, is the entire

31

event begun in Jordan, completed on Calvary, and proclaimed in the resurrection.

51 (*b*) Until that event was complete the new dispensation of the Spirit could not begin. Pentecost presupposes Calvary and Easter (John 7.39). It is when the baptism of Jesus is complete that he can and does return to bestow upon his disciples the gift of the Spirit so that they in turn can become part of the mission from the Father and agents of his liberating power for those held in the grip of sin (John 20.22-3). And those who accept the call to follow Jesus are in turn incorporated by baptism in water in the triune name to become, by the indwelling of the Spirit, part of his liberating mission, made members together in the one body of Christ and acknowledged as children of the one Father (Acts 2.38; Rom. 8.14-17; 1 Cor. 12.13; Gal. 3.27). In our water-baptism we are brought sacramentally into union with the once-for-all baptism of Jesus on behalf of all mankind, ourselves and our children, and we claim the Father's promised gift of the Spirit.

52 (*c*) Baptism means, therefore, the participation of believers through the Spirit in what Christ has done for us and continues to do for us as he shares with us his communion with the Father and his mission to the world. It is thus incorporation into Christ, into a life of dying and rising with Christ (Rom. 6.1-11; 2 Cor. 4.7-15), sharing with him his ministry as the servant in the fellowship of his sufferings and the power of his resurrection, immersed in his liberating death where our sins are buried, where the 'old Adam' is crucified with Christ and the power of sin is broken. In baptism Christ identifies us with himself in his victory over the powers of evil, his ministry of reconciliation, and we believe that

we shall be one with him in the final resurrection. The one baptism is therefore our common incorporation into Christ, into this common life of shared worship and mission in him. It is the visible and effective sign and seal of that gracious work of the Spirit by which the Church is constituted.

53 (*d*) Baptism, by which Christ incorporates us into his life, death and resurrection, is thus, in the strictest sense, constitutive of the Church. It is not simply one of the Church's practices. It is an event in which God, by engaging us to himself, opens to us the life of faith and builds the Church. As Jesus was baptized, anointed by the Spirit from the Father, and declared to be the Son, so we are incorporated into the Church in the triune name, and are commanded: 'Go therefore and make disciples of all nations, baptizing them in the name of the Father and of the Son and of the Holy Spirit, teaching them to observe all that I have commanded you' (Matt. 28.19f.). Baptism is therefore never an uninterpreted action. As the voice from heaven proclaimed its meaning, so in preaching we proclaim in the power of the Spirit that 'this Jesus is the Christ', and in every baptism proclaim his name. Word and action are inseparable.

54 (*e*) The gospel invites from us the response of faith and repentance. When Christ vicariously submitted for us to the baptism of repentance, and accepted the consequences of human sin for us on the cross, it was not to exonerate us from the need for personal faith and repentance but to bring us to faith and repentance in the assurance that our sins are forgiven. Hence we must not separate baptism from faith and repentance. With all Christians we acknowledge the necessity of faith for the reception of the salvation set forth and embodied

in baptism. Our practice of infant baptism does not deny this, but rests upon the priority of what Christ has done once for all on behalf of the whole human family, and upon the conviction that 'the act of God in baptism finds its response of faith not only from the one baptized but also from the community of faith which includes the child's family. It is in this community, the Church, that a child develops as a person to the point where, later in time, he or she personally appropriates the response of faith' (WARC-BWA Report, 1973-7, Section VI).

55 It has to be confessed that in both our communions many baptized as infants have not in fact been led to make this personal appropriation. This has caused some who have come in later life to a living faith to ask for a second baptism on the ground that their baptism as infants was invalid. We are agreed, on the one hand, that this situation is a summons to re-examine our baptismal discipline and the care given to the Christian nurture of those baptized as infants. On the other hand we must insist that the call for a second baptism rests on a failure to understand that baptism is primarily the work of God in Christ. The apostolic writers speak of baptism with the utmost realism (Rom. 6.3ff.; 1 Cor. 6.11; Col. 3.12; Titus 3.5). Something irreversible was done when we were baptized: God, through the Spirit, drew us into the death and new life of his Son. But, like the baptism of Jesus, our baptism is not an end but a beginning. We are committed to follow Jesus in his engagement with the prince of this world. Our baptism is to be completed, as his was, by going the way of the cross. This is true whether we are baptized as adults or as infants. It is therefore possible to betray our baptism – to become apostate. It is not possible either to undo it or to repeat it.

56   As the baptism of Jesus was a beginning, prophetically embracing both its fulfilment in his ministry and its consummation in his death and resurrection, so the baptism of a Christian is likewise the beginning of a process. It looks forward to a life of developing discipleship in the continual offering up of life itself until at death we say by grace: 'Father, into your hands I commit my spirit'. There is considerable debate within both our communions about the conditions under which baptism should be administered, and the ways in which its fulfilment in mature discipleship should be marked. We are agreed that baptism is the essential rite of initiation into the life in Christ; that baptism is in water and the Spirit; and that it is the beginning of a life in Christ which has to grow and reach full maturity. Beyond this there are matters which are the subject of discussion. While both communions have traditionally baptized the infant children of Christian parents, there is discussion within our churches of the propriety of this. Some churches permit both infant baptism and the postponement of baptism until the child of Christian parents can make a personal confession of faith. All our churches, moreover, seek to bring those baptized in infancy to confirmation or an analogous rite in which prayer is made for strengthening by the Holy Spirit (with or without the imposition of hands), and the person concerned is admitted to the full responsibilities of membership.

57   Further there are differences between and within our traditions about the meaning and conditions of membership. These have been shaped not only by our differing theological confessions but even more by our differing relations to society. Even in those parts of the world which were formerly identified as 'Christendom',

it is no longer possible seriously to think of baptism as the customary rite immediately following birth, and of confirmation as the customary rite marking entry into adult status – even though these ideas persist in some places. All our churches are, and increasingly know themselves to be, in a missionary situation. Membership in the Church, therefore, is seen as distinct from membership in the civil society. In this respect our two communions share a common experience. There are indeed places where baptism may result in a person being cast out of his society, and even in his death. But separation is for the sake of a true solidarity, for Christ was cast out in order to draw all humankind into its true unity. We are being reminded again that baptism is into his death. There is a difference between our two communions in the way they define membership. Reformed churches have tended to define it primarily as membership in a local congregation, while Anglicans, by the practice of episcopal confirmation, have emphasized membership in the wider church. These emphases, however, are complementary rather than contradictory and require further exploration by our churches.

58   The scene is further complicated by the rise of the 'charismatic' movement within both our communions, which has led to an emphasis on recognizable tokens of the Spirit's presence as the proper mark of full membership. In some places this leads to a denial of the validity of the baptism received in infancy and the demand for baptism anew. On the one hand we must welcome and cherish all the signs in our time of a new quickening by the Spirit in the lives of members. On the other hand we must steadily maintain the eschatological perspective which we have tried to outline in this Report. Our

perspective is controlled by the hope of God's perfect Kingdom. Our life in Christ is a growing up, a journeying towards that blessed consummation. Whether we speak of the baptism of infants or of believers, or of a 'second blessing' by the Spirit, none of these is the end of the journey. All of these are markers pointing the way towards a goal which lies beyond our sight, but is known and cherished in faith.

59   These differences are for the most part not between but within our communions. A report such as ours cannot pretend to resolve them. In part they arise from a fresh sense of the missionary calling of the Church, and are therefore to be welcomed. We believe that, in the perspective of a dynamic understanding of the Church as the provisional incorporation of humankind into Christ, while not all our differences are resolved, we can together acknowledge our one baptism as a gift of God's sheer grace to those who can never be more than beginners in their grasp of it, as God's calling to grow up into the fullness of Christ and as the sign of God's purpose of redemption for all humankind through the passion and victory of Christ.

60   (*f*) At the heart of the New Testament teaching about baptism lies the biblical concept of 'the one for the many' and 'the many in the one' – that the one Christ gave his life for the many and that the many have their life in the one Christ. In the Old Testament God elected the one nation of Israel to be a royal priesthood on behalf of all nations, that in Abraham all nations might be blessed. This election of Israel to the royal priesthood found its fulfilment in the incarnation, in Christ's anointing by the Spirit to be the high priest of humanity, that God's purpose for all nations might be brought to fulfilment in and through him. God's

purpose in the gospel is to restore our true humanity in Christ, that what was lost in Adam might be restored in Christ as the head of the race, the head of a new humanity. When Christ, therefore, calls the Church to be a royal priesthood and baptizes the one Church by the one Spirit at Pentecost, it is that the Church may be the one people of God for all nations, sent out to preach the gospel and baptize the nations, that God may call the whole of humanity to become his people. It is in these terms that we understand baptism – the baptism of Christ for us and our common baptism into Christ. When Christ was baptized for us in the waters of Jordan and in blood on the cross, we were baptized into his baptism. When he died we died in him. When he was buried we were buried in him. When he rose we rose in him. And now our life is hid with Christ in God. 'For the love of Christ controls us, because we are convinced that one has died for all; therefore all have died. And he died for all, that those who live might live no longer for themselves but for him who for their sake died and was raised' (2 Cor. 5.14f.). This Christ, the one for many, baptizes the Church by the Spirit, that as one body we may participate with him in his ministry of reconciliation, to restore to all nations their true humanity as the children of one father (2 Cor. 5.18–21).

61 (g) This understanding of our common baptism has very great practical consequences. If we are as realistic about baptism as the apostolic writers are, then we are already by our baptism one body, and the continued separation of our two communions is a public denial of what we are already in Christ. Moreover, there are consequences beyond these ecclesiastical ones. In the one man Jesus we see our common humanity taken up, redeemed and given back to us so that we can share

it together – Jew and Gentile, man and woman, slave and free, rich and poor, white and black. Fidelity to our baptism commits us to affirm in word and practice the full, equal and God-given humanity of every person, to embody that affirmation in our public and political life, and to oppose and resist all that denies this shared humanity. Our baptism commits us to follow Jesus on the way of the cross, in warfare against the world, the flesh and the devil, until everything will be subject to the Father and own Jesus as lord.

The Eucharist

62   As in our understanding of baptism, so with reference to the Eucharist, it is in the missionary and eschatological context that we are enabled to see beyond the things which create divisions between and within our two communions. While there is, and has always been, a very great measure of agreement between us on the doctrine of the Eucharist, it would be idle to deny that divergent practices, and, even more, divergent styles of spirituality in regard to the Eucharist, have often made mutual understanding difficult. With regard to these differences, we acknowledge that we have much to receive from each other. We seek here to state what we hold in common.

63   (*a*) Baptism and Eucharist rest alike upon the finished work of Christ in his incarnation, death, resurrection and ascension. Our baptism is a participation in the baptism of Jesus begun in Jordan and consummated on Calvary. By the same token when we are obedient to the words and deeds of Jesus on the eve of his passion, our celebration of the Eucharist is a

participation in the benefits of his death and resurrection. Both have, therefore, their basis in the one work of Jesus, accomplished once for all, proclaimed and made effective for us by the continuing work of the Spirit. Our baptism engages us to follow Jesus on the way of the cross; when we share in the Eucharist Christ renews that same engagement with us and enables us to renew our engagement to him. He feeds his pilgrim people. Like the Passover, the Eucharist is to be received as provision for an urgent journey (Exod. 12.11). Christ fulfils the Eucharist in his people when the communicants go into the world to their daily tasks as his servants and as witnesses to the Kingdom of God. This makes no light claim upon our discipleship. As the Lima report puts it: 'The eucharist shows us that our behavior is inconsistent in the face of the reconciling presence of God in human history: we are placed under continual judgment by the persistence of unjust relationships of all kinds in our society, the manifold divisions on account of human pride, material interest and power politics . . .' (BEM, p. 14, para. 20).

64 (*b*) At every celebration of the Eucharist we rehearse the deeds and words of Jesus on the night of his passion. At that moment too there was urgency. It was a moment of separation when Jesus had to go alone to his death, leaving the disciples behind. But his leaving them was in order that, having won the victory, he might return to lead them on the way, the 'new and living way' which he himself is (Heb. 10.19ff.; John 14.1-6). He must go alone, but it is in order that they may follow afterwards (John 13.36). So it is 'for their sake' that he consecrates himself to the Father, in order that 'they may also be consecrated in the truth' (John 17.19). And in this moment of urgency, of separation,

and of perplexity, Jesus gives to the disciples the bread and wine of their shared meal with the words, 'This is my body', 'This is my blood', and adds the solemn command: 'Do this in remembrance of me'. This is the visible enactment of what is expressed in the words of the consecration prayer as given by St John (John 17.18). The disciples, who do not now understand the words or the intention of Jesus, are made participants in the action of Jesus to which he must now go alone, and they are commanded to do this thing through which he will become present with them and unite them with him in his consecration to the Father. And it was as the disciples obeyed this command that they came to know that he was alive with them in his risen life (Luke 24.35). In this sense we must say that the Eucharist is constitutive of the Church because in it Christ unites the disciples with himself.

65 (*c*) The Eucharist is a memorial (*anamnesis*) of the unique sacrifice of Christ. This is more than a mere mental action of recollection. It is the 'living and effective sign of Christ's sacrifice, accomplished once for all on the cross, and still operative on behalf of all humankind' (BEM, p. 11, para. 5). When we 'do this' in obedience to his command, we know that his words are true: 'This is my body. This is my blood.' We know that in the action of the Eucharist Christ is truly present to share his risen life with us and to unite us with himself in his self-offering to the Father, the one full, perfect and sufficient sacrifice which he alone can offer and has offered once for all. And as he, the risen Lord, ever lives at the Father's side to make intercession for us, so we, united with him, offer up in this action of the Eucharist our intercessions for the Church and the world.

66   We have frequently been divided in our understanding of this point because of a pervasive dualism
which separates what Scripture holds together – visible
and invisible, outward and inward, objective and subjec-
tive. We are of course all agreed that in the Eucharist
God is truly 'with us': that he joins us to himself in
Christ in and through created realities. There is a real
presence of Christ which 'does not depend upon the
faith of the individual', even though, 'to discern the
body and blood of Christ faith is required' (BEM,
p. 12, para. 13). The trouble begins, however, when we
commence to argue whether this presence is associated
with the outward, visible elements of bread and wine, or
whether it is an inward, invisible presence received in
the heart through faith. The fact is that both statements
are true; neither should be so asserted as to exclude the
other. 'Eucharistic doctrine must hold together these
two movements since in the Eucharist, the sacrament of
the New Covenant, Christ gives himself to his people so
that they may receive him through faith' (ARCIC
Elucidations, para. 7).

67   There has also been a destructive polarization in
our common history between emphasis on the preached
word and emphasis on the sacrament. This is to put
asunder what is given to us in Scripture and in the
gospel as one. The gospel is news of the word made
flesh. The preached word is an *anamnesis* of Christ
just as is the eucharistic meal. Hence 'the celebration of
the eucharist properly includes the proclamation of the
word' (BEM, p. 12, para. 12). Both word and sacrament
have their actualization in the presence of the risen
Lord. Our two traditions have tended to emphasize the
one side or the other of this single reality – the word
acted or the word proclaimed. We need each other's

help to restore at this point the unity which should never have been lost (see paras. 8 and 39 above).

68 (*d*) Our being united to Christ in his offering of himself to the Father is a work of the Holy Spirit. The prayer of invocation (*epiklesis*) is therefore a proper part of the eucharistic action. 'The Church prays to the Father for the gift of the Holy Spirit in order that the eucharistic event may be a reality: the real presence of the crucified and risen Christ giving his life for all humanity' (BEM, p. 13, para. 13). The Eucharist is a making present of the once-for-all sacrifice of Christ. Joined to Christ in that sacrifice, the Church makes an acceptable offering of itself in thanksgiving to the Father. We therefore invoke the gift of the Spirit from the Father to sanctify both us and the elements of bread and wine, so that in our eating and drinking we may be united with the one sacrifice of Jesus. 'Sanctified by his Spirit, the Church, through, with and in God's Son Jesus Christ, offers itself to the Father. It thereby becomes a living sacrifice of thanksgiving through which God is publicly praised' (WARC/RC, Section 81).

69 (*e*) The presence of the Spirit is the foretaste, pledge and first-fruits of God's coming Kingdom. At every Eucharist the Church looks forward to the consummation of that reign. 'In this union of the Church on earth with the risen and ascended Christ, which he continues to sustain through its eucharistic communion with him, the Church is enabled by grace to participate in his reconciling mission to the world. Christ and his Church share in this in different ways: Christ vicariously as Mediator and Redeemer, the Church as the community of the redeemed to whom he has entrusted the ministry of reconciliation (2 Cor. 5.18), and stewardship of the mysteries (cf. 1 Cor. 4.1). "As often as you eat this

bread and drink this cup, you proclaim the Lord's death till he comes" (1 Cor. 11.26). Thus precisely because the mission of the Church is grounded in, and sustained through the eucharistic communion with Christ, [the Church] is sent out by Christ into all the nations and all ages in the service of the Gospel, in reliance upon his promise that he will be present to it always to the end of the world' (ibid., Section 86).

70   (*f*) The Eucharist which unites us with Christ and feeds us with his own life in his body and blood, unites us at the same time with one another and with the whole company of Christ's people in every age and place. It is therefore a condition for participation in the Eucharist that we have forgiven one another and are in love and charity with our neighbours. Participation in the Eucharist commits us to the ceaseless search for reconciliation among all for whom Christ died, and is incompatible with the exclusion of any person on grounds of race, sex, social distinction or culture as well as with the refusal to share material resources given by God for the benefit of all. In relation to all that divides Christians at the Lord's table we have to ponder the grave words of St Paul about those who eat and drink judgement to themselves (1 Cor. 11.17–32).

71   (*g*) Along with baptism, the Eucharist is funda-mental to and constitutive of the life of the Church. It is the sacrament given to the Church by her Lord for the continual renewal of her life in him. It is therefore the proper form of worship for the weekly assembling of the Church on the Lord's day, the day of resurrection, the birthday of the new creation. In neither of our traditions were the first reformers successful in per-suading the great mass of Christians that it was their privilege to share in the Eucharist every Sunday. Recent

decades have seen in both our communions a recovery of the integral relationship between Sunday worship and the Eucharist, but recovery is far from universal. We believe that it should be accepted as the norm in both our traditions.

72 (h) Churches as a whole have long been divided on the question whether participation in the Eucharist should be open to all the baptized including infants and children, or whether it should be limited to those able to understand a course of teaching about its meaning. In common with the rest of Western Christendom, our two traditions have followed the second alternative, but in both there is a growing questioning of it. Some in both our traditions have been impressed by the example of Eastern churches which receive baptized infants to communion with their parents. It is indeed difficult to defend the practice of admitting children to baptism while denying them the Eucharist. However, all of us would wish to affirm the need for a rite in which those baptized as infants, whether they have been accepted as communicants or not, are enabled, after due preparation, to make their own confession of faith and commitment to Christ, and are renewed by the grace of God through a further invocation of the Spirit, so that they can commit themselves freely and deliberately to share in God's mission to the world. The remaining questions about the relation of confirmation to baptism are not, in our judgement, such as to prevent mutual recognition of one another's members by the churches of our two communions. There are, however, questions concerning the ministry which still prevent such mutual recognition, and we turn now to consider these.

IV MINISTRY IN THE CHURCH

Ministry of the Church and in the Church

73 The Church is sent by God to witness in the world to his unlimited grace. Only in this double perspective of mission and of the new life in Christ experienced as the free gift of grace can ministry in the Church and the ministry of the Church be adequately understood. The Church as a whole, and all ministry within and on behalf of the Church, have one source in the action of the Father in sending the Son into the world anointed by the Spirit to announce and embody God's blessed reign over all humankind and all creation. For the fulfilment of this mission Jesus called others to follow him and – in particular – appointed twelve 'to be with him and that he might send them out to preach and to have authority to cast out demons' (Mark 3.14f.). After his final victory over the powers of evil, Jesus returned to assure these disciples that he was still with them, giving them the gift of his peace, sending them into the world to continue his mission, giving to them his Spirit, and entrusting to them the ministry of release from sin and reconciliation with the Father (John 20.19–23). As he thus commissioned them, he showed them the scars of his passion, a reminder to them of the way his mission went and theirs must go – the way of the cross. The kingship of God and his victory over the powers of evil will be made manifest to the world only under the sign of the cross.

74 The company gathered behind closed doors on that first Easter evening was the Church in embryo. It is to the whole Church that the commission is given and it is

to the whole Church that the gift of the Spirit is made. The Church as a whole is constituted by this act of sending and anointing. It exists, therefore, not for itself but for the glory of God in the fulfilment of that mission for which Jesus was sent from the Father. The primary ministry is that of the risen Christ himself, and we are enabled to participate in it by the power of the Spirit. His ministry is entrusted to sinful men and women and it is only as debtors to grace that we can fulfil it. The mission of the Church is an overflow of the grace of God. It is only as those whose sins have been freely forgiven that we can be the bearers to others of God's gift of forgiveness. This ministry is exercised by and through the entire membership of the Church in the course of their daily work in the world. Every member of the Church, therefore, abiding in Christ, shares in this ministry.

75 The same company gathered in that shuttered room was also the ministry in embryo. Those who were there commissioned and anointed were sent to call others to be with Jesus and, in their turn, to be sent. The disciples are to 'make disciples of all nations' (Matt. 28.19). As they have heard and obeyed the call of Jesus, 'Follow me', so they in turn are to call others, and these others are, in their turn, both to 'be with Jesus' and to 'be sent' in the service of God's Kingdom.

76 Thus from the very beginning there is a pattern of ministerial leadership in the life of the Church. It is to the whole Church that the commission is given, but the Church was never an unstructured aggregate of individual believers out of which a ministerial structure had to develop. On the contrary there was from the beginning a pattern of calling and following. The first disciples are both the first followers and the first apostles sent to call

others to follow. And this calling is always to a double relationship with Jesus: to be with him and to be sent. As he sends them he promises to be with them – to the ends of the earth and the end of the world (Matt. 28.19f.). Leadership in the Church means leading others into the company of Jesus so that – in him and by the working of the Spirit – their lives may be offered to the Father, and also leading others into the world to challenge the dominion of evil in the name of Christ and in the power of the Spirit. This double calling finds its unity in the cross which was at the same time Jesus' total offering of himself to the Father on behalf of all humankind, and the decisive victory of God's Kingdom over the dominion of evil. Ministerial leadership in the Church may therefore be defined as following Jesus in the way of the cross so that others in turn may be enabled to follow in the same way.

77   If ministry is understood in this way, the Church is protected from two opposite tendencies: on the one hand, the tendency to regard the ordained ministry as something separate from the Church, having its being independently of the whole body; on the other hand, the tendency to regard the ordained ministry as something created by the Church in the course of historical development. The Scriptures show us that 'the Church has never been without persons holding specific authority and responsibility' (BEM, p. 21, para. 9). Certainly, however, the varied forms of ordained ministry have evolved in the course of history. On this three things may be said: (i) The particular ministerial structures which are now embodied in our different communions cannot claim the direct authority of Scripture. The New Testament cannot be held to prescribe a three-fold ministry of bishops, priests and deacons, a presbyterian or congregational form of government, or the primacy of

the see of Rome. All attempts to read off one divinely authorized form of ministry from the New Testament are futile. (ii) The Church is a living body which should combine continuity of tradition with adaptation to new situations under the guidance of the Holy Spirit. (iii) Not all the developments of the past nineteen centuries are to be regarded as divinely sanctioned simply because they have occurred. The ministerial forms which we inherit have been developed in the course of the Church's missionary advance through the centuries and among the nations. They are neither to be treated as immutable because they exist, nor to be rejected because they are not explicitly authorized by Scripture. Our duty is first to receive and cherish them with gratitude, and then to learn, as those before us have done, to adapt and reform them under the guidance of the Spirit in faithfulness to the apostolic witness, and in accordance with the missionary needs of our day.

78   In both our traditions a wide variety of words is used to describe the work of the ordained ministry. Anglicans widely use the word 'priest', but this has never been used in the Reformed tradition. Both our communions make use of the pastoral image of the ministry, but it is often used in a way which contradicts its missionary thrust. 'Shepherd' in the Old Testament is the familiar title for the kings and other rulers who led their people, ruled them, guarded them and went before them into battle. The Good Shepherd in Jesus' language is the one who is willing for the sake of the sheep to meet the attacking wolves and give his life in the combat (John 10.7-15). And when Jesus entrusts to Peter the pastoral care of his flock he immediately tells Peter that it will entail learning to follow him on the way that leads to the cross (John 21.15-19).

79   The word priest is used in the New Testament of Christ himself, and of his whole body, the Church. The New Testament does not use the word 'priest' to designate any Christian minister. The word came into use early in the Church's history to designate the bishop, and was then extended to his presbyters. Anglicans, in common with most Christians, have continued this usage. The Reformed, in common with other churches of the Reformation, abandoned the usage on account of its connection with a particular doctrine of eucharistic sacrifice, and also because it was not authorized by Scripture. We are, however, agreed that since it is acknowledged that the whole Church is called to be in Christ a priestly people (1 Peter 2.5,9), and since ministers are called to lead, enable and equip the Church for this priestly office, the priestly nature of the ministry cannot be denied. We can accept all the following words of the WCC statement: 'Ordained ministers are related, as are all Christians, both to the priesthood of Christ and to the priesthood of the Church. But they may appropriately be called priests because they fill a particular priestly service by strengthening and building up the royal and prophetic priesthood of the faithful through word and sacraments, through their prayers of intercession, and through their pastoral guidance of the community' (BEM, p. 23, para. 17). We recognize however that the word 'priest', used of an ordained minister, has acquired overtones which render it unacceptable to many Christians. We would not in such circumstances expect the word to be universally used. We would, however, wish to insist that while the word may appropriately be used, other words, such as pastor, presbyter, minister, are no less appropriate.

Ordination, Authority, Continuity

80   Those who may thus be called 'priests' exercise their priestly ministry neither apart from the priesthood of the whole body, nor by derivation from the priesthood of the whole body, but by virtue of their participation, in company with the whole body, in the priestly ministry of the risen Christ, and as leaders, examples and enablers for the priestly ministry of the whole body in virtue of the special calling and equipment given to them in ordination. The one so ordained is called to be a focus of unity for the whole body. Ordination is the act which constitutes and acknowledges this special ministry of representation and leadership within the life of the Church both locally and universally. In the act of ordination, the Church in Christ prays to the Father to grant his Spirit to the one ordained for the office and work to which that person is called, accompanying the act with a sacramental sign which specifies by the imposition of hands the one for whom the prayer is made, and – in faith that the prayer is heard – commits to the person ordained the authority to act representatively for the universal Church in the ways proper to that particular office.

81   The Spirit gives gifts to all members of the Church, equipping them for many kinds of ministry. All are called to be good stewards of God's varied gifts (1 Peter 4.10). But not all are ordained. The New Testament does not give us direct guidance as to who should be ordained. From very early times ordination has been connected with the Eucharist. In the Eucharist Christ himself is present in his fullness, and the company which shares in it is therefore the catholic Church in that place. It is not the branch of an organization of which the centre is elsewhere, for where Christ is, there is the

catholic Church – God's gathering together of the people into their true Head. But even in the New Testament itself we find that a problem arises where groups of Christians propose to celebrate the supper in separation from their fellow-members. This seems to be the situation envisaged in Paul's remonstrance to the Corinthians (1 Cor. 11.17-22). How is the distinction to be made between the Eucharist in which Christ is present in the midst of his universal Church, and the celebration of a divisive group which is in the Apostle's word 'not the Lord's supper' (v. 20)? This was a practical question which had to be answered. At an early stage Ignatius of Antioch formulated the answer in the general provision that a 'valid' Eucharist is one presided over by the one acknowledged by the congregation and by neighbouring congregations as its leader, or by one authorized by him.

82   It is clear, on the one hand, that this is a matter of the harmonious ordering of the life of the Church. The one who presides does so, not in virtue of a different relationship to the life of the risen Christ from the rest of the body, but because – as a matter of order – he has been so authorized. But, on the other hand, it is clear that this ordering is of central importance for the very life of the Church. It arises from a genuine concern that what is celebrated should truly be the Lord's supper. For order is love in regulative operation, and love is the fundamental reality of the Church's being.

83   It is in this context that we must consider what is sometimes called 'lay presidency' at the Eucharist, which has been at various times a matter of dispute between Anglican and Reformed Christians. The practice of 'lay celebration' has sometimes been advocated because it was held to be a necessary witness to the

'priesthood of all believers'. This advocacy clearly rests on a misunderstanding, since it implies that it is the president who is alone the priest. The practice thus contradicts the doctrine which it is intended to support. On the other hand there have been and there still are situations where, because of a shortage of ordained ministers, or because of very rapid missionary advance, there are congregations which must either have the Eucharist without an ordained minister, or else have no Eucharist at all except on rare occasions. In some cases it may be said that this indicates a lack of proper foresight on the part of the Church's leadership, but this observation does not meet the immediate pastoral need. Reformed churches have therefore frequently taken the view that a lay person should be given authority by the Church to preside at the Eucharist in such circumstances. This is justified on the ground that the orderly modification of normal practice may meet particular pastoral needs, and fulfil the intention which the general practice is intended to serve. The general rule should remain that the president at the Eucharist should be the person who has, by ordination, received the authority so to preside, and the Church ought to order its affairs in such a way that this proper rule may be kept. The presidency of the ordained person does not depend upon his possessing a priesthood which others lack; it depends upon the good ordering which is essential to the life of the Church as it exercises corporately the priesthood given to it by the one who is alone the good High Priest.

84 We associate ourselves with the following exposition of the threefold nature of ordination as given in the WCC statement:

> *(a)* Ordination is an invocation to God that the new minister

be given the power of the Holy Spirit in the new relation which is established between this minister and the local community and, by intention, the Church universal. The otherness of God's initiative, of which the ordained ministry is a sign, is here acknowledged in the act of ordination itself. 'The Spirit blows where it will' (John 3.3). The invocation of the Spirit implies the absolute dependence upon God for the outcome of the Church's prayer. This means the Spirit may set new forces in motion and open new possibilities 'far more abundantly than all that we ask or think' (Eph. 3.20).

(b) Ordination is a sign of the granting of this prayer by the Lord who gives the gift of the ordained ministry. Although the outcome of the Church's *epiklesis* depends on the freedom of God, the Church ordains in confidence that God, being faithful to his promise in Christ, enters sacramentally into contingent, historical forms of human relationship and uses them for his purpose. Ordination is a sign performed in faith that the spiritual relationship signified is present in, with and through the words spoken, the gestures made and the forms employed.

(c) Ordination is an acknowledgement by the Church of the gifts of the Spirit in the one ordained, and a commitment by both the Church and the ordinand to the new relationship. By receiving the new minister in the act of ordination, the congregation acknowledges the minister's gifts and commits itself to be open towards these gifts. Likewise those ordained offer their gifts to the Church and commit themselves to the burden and opportunity of new authority and responsibility. At the same time, they enter into a collegial relationship with other ministers.

(BEM, pp. 30–1, paras. 42–4)

85 In the ministry of the word and sacrament the whole Church is again and again enabled to receive forgiveness and to renew its participation in Christ's ministry in the world. The minister as leader has a representative character, to act as 'the one on behalf of

the many', so that the whole Church is represented in his person as he carries on his heart the concerns of all his people. He does not act in his own name, but in the name of Christ, and in the name of the whole body of Christ, so that he is at once the mouthpiece of our Lord and the mouthpiece of his flock. This is acknowledged in ordination, both in the case of those who ordain and of those who are ordained. Those who ordain act in the name of Christ and of the whole catholic Church, and the one who is ordained is set apart to act as a minister, not of one denomination, but of the one body of Christ.

86   Ordination involves as part of its essential nature the entrusting of authority to the ordained person to act focally and representatively for the whole Church. The ordained ministry has therefore always been seen as both a sign of unity in the Church and a means of maintaining it. For the same reason the ordained ministry is inevitably the point at which issues arising from the disunity of the Church are most sharply focused. Ministry, which is properly a sign of unity and continuity, has become the most obvious symbol of division.

87   We confess one holy catholic and apostolic Church. In the ordination rites of both our traditions, we make our invocation to the Father in the name of Christ and therefore intend that the ordination is to the ministry of his universal Church carrying an authorization universally valid. In fact, because we are divided, the prayers are not the prayers of the whole Church and the authorization is not acknowledged by the whole Church. In particular our two communions are divided at this point because of different views about the role of the continuity of ordination in signifying and safe-

guarding unity.

88   The Church lives in historic continuity from
Christ's coming until his coming again. This continuity
is grounded in the gift to the Church of the Spirit
through whom we participate in Christ's continuing
ministry. In maintaining this continuity the Church
depends upon the written Scriptures, the sacraments of
baptism and the Eucharist, the ecumenical creeds and
the continuing transmission of teaching and practice
from generation to generation, wherever Christian
parents and teachers hand on to their children and
pupils that which they have received. In this process of
transmission there is always the possibility of distortion.
As a corrective of this, the early Church prized the
continuity of public teaching in the great centres of
Christian life focused in the personal teaching ministry
of the bishops. This succession of public episcopal
ministry could be appealed to as a ground of assurance
that what was being taught was the authentic message
of Jesus and the apostles. The acceptance of the canon
of the apostolic writings in the New Testament provided
a written record to which this appeal could be made.

89   Related to this appeal, but distinct from it, is the
appeal to the continuity of succession in ordination.
In so far as ordination involves committing of authority
to certain persons to act representatively for the whole
Church, it is obvious that it can only be properly performed by those who have received authority thereto.
Churches normally decline to acknowledge ordinations
carried out by persons who have not been authorized by
the Church to act in this way. Historic continuity of
office-holders is, in fact, the normal way by which the
continuity of any corporate body is secured and signified. Anglicans preserve this continuity or succession

through episcopal ordination; in the Reformed tradition it is preserved through ministerial ordination.

90   But ordination is not simply the committing of authority by the Church. It is first of all an invocation to the Father asking for the gift of the Spirit to the ordinand. The answering of that prayer lies within the sovereign freedom of the Father to whom the prayer is addressed. In our divided state the prayers which we offer are not the unanimous prayer of the catholic Church. Nevertheless, it is not open to us to say that the answer of the Father is defective. Our two communions, in common with others, have been led through our participation in the ecumenical movement to acknowledge that ordinations which were defective, both in that they were the prayers of divided churches and in that the authority of those ordaining was not the authority of the universal Church, have been acknowledged and blessed by God who, being faithful to his promises, has entered sacramentally into these acts and used them for his gracious purpose. We have been led to acknowledge this in humble gratitude, and thus to acknowledge the reality of one another's churchly life. But this gives us no ground for concluding that the historic continuity of ordinations is an irrelevance. On the contrary it is an element in the proper visible form of the Church's unity in space and time, to the end of the age and the ends of the earth. We therefore affirm that the ways by which our separated churches are brought into unity must be such as to ensure (*a*) that the reality of God's gift of ministry to the churches in their separation is unambiguously acknowledged; and (*b*) that the continuity of succession in ordination with the undivided Church is – so far as lies in our power – visibly restored and maintained.

Patterns of Ministry

91 The patterns of the ordained ministry in the Anglican and Reformed traditions are on the surface very different. Beneath the differences, however, there can be discerned a common pattern which involves, in each local church, a chief pastor who works with a body of colleagues and a staff of helpers or assistants to forward the work of Christ in Church and world. This pattern first appeared in the early Church's division of the ordained ministry into the work of bishop, presbyter and deacon. While the tendency in both our traditions has been to truncate this pattern by effectively reducing the orders to two (bishop–priest, minister–elder), the classic pattern reflects an ordering which developed and was found appropriate in the life of the Church – those, namely, of pastor, a collegial association for the pastor, and pastoral assistants to carry out ministry in the world. This threefold pattern cannot claim to be the only one authorized in Scripture. The various authors of the New Testament point rather to a variety of patterns which existed in the earliest period of the Church. But the threefold pattern eventually prevailed and was generally adopted by the Church. The large majority of churches have maintained it in one form or another to the present day.

92 In both our traditions this pattern has suffered deformation in the course of history. We believe, however, that it should be accepted in some form for the sake of the unity and continuity of the Church, both locally and universally, and for the sake of its missionary calling. But if it is to serve these ends, the ministry must conform to that of Christ. Christ has given the gift of ministries to the Church 'to equip the

saints for the work of ministry, for building up the body
of Christ, until we all attain to the unity of the faith
and of the knowledge of the Son of God, to mature
manhood, to the measuure of the stature of the fullness
of Christ' (Eph. 4.12f.). To the extent that ministry
conforms to Christ, it reflects the character of God as
revealed in the incarnation. As God in Christ deals with
us in a personal way, so all ministry must have a *personal* character, providing in a specific person a focus
for the unity and witness of the community. As God
calls us into a reconciled fellowship, so all ministry must
have a *collegial* character – exercised not by one person
alone but in shared responsibility with colleagues. As
the Church is the body of Christ quickened by the
Spirit, so the ministry must have a communal character,
so that every member is enabled to exercise the gifts
which the Spirit gives and so that the whole community
is, as far as possible, associated in the process of teaching and decision making. And as the work of Christ was
that of the servant Lord who gave his life a ransom for
many, so these three characteristics must combine in a
ministry of service to the world for which Christ died.

93   How can the ministry of bishops, presbyters and
deacons fulfil these three requirements? In the beginning
these three ministries were the ministries of the local
church. The bishop was the shepherd and leader of the
local community; he presided over the celebration of
the Eucharist. He was surrounded by a college of
presbyters who with him had the responsibility of
teaching, preaching and leadership. He was assisted by
deacons who gave special attention to the diaconal
witness of the community. Evidence for this pattern
can be found in the letters of Ignatius. As the Church
grew, congregations multiplied in each place. This led

to a shift of responsibilities. The bishop became the leader of several congregations while the presbyters became the shepherds of these congregations. In this way, and no doubt for good reasons, the bishop's office gradually became a regional one. It is evident that by this shift of responsibilities the balance between the personal and collegial dimensions of the exercise of the ordained ministry was destroyed. The question therefore arises for both our communions: how can this balance be restored at all levels of the Church's life? As the churches of our two families try to answer this question, the movement towards unity will become easier.

94 In their attempt to return to the origins of the Church, the Reformers of the sixteenth century reintroduced the threefold ministry in the local church. In each congregation of the Reformed tradition there was to be a pastor for the proclamation of the word of God and the administration of the sacraments. He was to be surrounded by a group of elders and deacons. Most churches in the Reformed tradition adhere to this pattern today, though the diaconate as a separate ministry has not been maintained in all places. In the Congregational tradition, however, lay leadership in the local church is normally entrusted to deacons, not elders. At the regional level the government is exercised by presbyters or representative groups elected by synods. The participation of the community finds expression at the local level through church assemblies and at the regional level through representative synods or councils in both the Presbyterian and Congregational traditions. Thus the personal, collegial and communal elements in the governance of the Church are adequately expressed at the local level. But the Reformed

churches have to ask themselves whether they attach enough importance to the personal dimension of the ordained ministry at the district or presbyterial level – that is to say, to the exercise of oversight in a particular way through one person together with and within a college.

95   In considering guidelines for the union of Anglican and Reformed churches, we call attention to the considerable variations of existing practice within both our communions. For example, in the Anglican communion the personal nature of episcopacy is substantially affected by the geographical size of the diocese and the number of people in the pastoral care of the bishop, and the office of deacon has taken new shape in Papua New Guinea and the United States; in some Reformed churches, elders are ordained for life and in some elected for a fixed term, while the name 'deacon' in Switzerland and Holland signifies a much fuller and more active form of service than is found in the Reformed diaconate in other parts of the world.

96   Keeping in mind what is said above (para. 92) about the personal, collegial and communal dimensions of ministry, we must consider what changes would be involved in Reformed practice if a moderator of presbytery or synod were to become a bishop-in-presbytery, and in Anglican practice if elders were to be introduced in congregations as a welcome embodiment of aspects of service which Anglicans recognize to have been present among the many activities of deacons in the history of the Church. As Anglican and Reformed churches unite in different parts of the world, there will be considerable variety in styles of ministry, corresponding to the variety that already exists within each communion. We expect Anglican–Reformed united churches to go on learning

from each other's experience, particularly in the initial decades, within the forms of mutually recognized ministry on the way to a universally recognized ministry. More detailed suggestions, no doubt limited in application because of the limitations of the membership of this Commission, are offered in Chapter V (paras. 110ff.).

97 Both our communions need to give urgent thought to the renewal of other forms of ministry. It is also perhaps necessary that both should consider afresh, in the light of contemporary circumstances, the relevance of the various ministries which are described in the New Testament under the names of prophets and evangelists. The role of the theologians in the life of the Church could well be considered afresh in the light of the teaching of the Geneva reformers on the 'doctors' (i.e. theological teachers) and of the teaching role of bishops.

Women and the Ordained Ministry

98 Our two traditions have not reached a common mind on the ordination of women to the threefold ministry. Practice varies in different cultural situations, but the Reformed churches in membership of WARC do not generally have theological objections to the ordination of women. In the course of the last fifty years most Reformed churches have begun to ordain women ministers, and they have taken this step out of conviction, and not because of a shortage of ministers. Where there is a theological objection to the ordination of women, it is usually based on biblical teaching emphasizing the headship of the male (see para. 103 below). However, even where there is no theological objection to women's ordination, it is not always accepted sociologically and emotionally. There is a

substantial minority of Reformed Christians who do not accept women ministers. Even where there are women ministers there has been little serious consideration of the distinctive contribution that women might make in the ordained ministry.

99 Of the twenty-seven Anglican provinces three (including two large ones) have ordained women priests, as have a few dioceses in other provinces. Of those provinces which do not ordain women eight have formally stated that they have no fundamental objections to the ordination of women to the priesthood, others have stated that they do have fundamental objections, and others have made no decision. At present there are no Anglican women bishops. Some provinces, who do not ordain women to the priesthood, have ordained women deacons, and others are considering doing so. This difference of theology and practice has not broken communion within the Anglican Communion. In the USA a few Anglicans have left the Episcopal Church because it has ordained women; but it has caused tension and heart-searching more widely.

100 As a joint commission of the two communions we can neither ignore this question, nor pretend to settle it. It is an issue which affects the unity of the Church both *within* our separate communions and *between* them. Differences of doctrine and practice on this issue have not yet substantially broken communion *within* either confessional family. However, it is the judgement of some that it was a major factor which told against the acceptance of the English Covenant proposals for unity between member churches of our two communions. It is clearly impossible for churches which exist in the same geographical area but which take

different stands on this issue to enter into complete union. It is therefore an issue the solution of which cannot be postponed much longer. We see no contradiction between the concept of the ordained ministries expressed in this document and the ordination of women. This matter is of equal concern to both traditions, and one on which we must work together.

101   The debate about the ordination of women to the ministry focuses upon three areas:

(*a*) Those opposed to the ordination of women argue that the force of nineteen centuries of tradition should not lightly be set aside; and that a decision on such an issue should not have been taken by one denomination on its own, but only by a universal Council of all the Churches. All those concerned for Christian unity will take this argument seriously, so long as it is not simply a device to block all discussion and change. How long is it right to expect those in favour of the ordination of women to wait, bearing in mind that there has not been a universally recognized General Council for a thousand years? If they are truly concerned for Christian unity, both those Churches who do ordain women and those who do not will desire urgently to meet and discover one another's motives and reasons for the stand they take on this issue.

102   (*b*) Some of those opposed to the ordination of women to the priesthood base their argument upon the maleness of Jesus, our one High Priest. They deny that a woman can preside at the Lord's Supper, since the president at the Eucharist in some respects re-presents Christ at the Last Supper. Those who support the ordination of women claim that the exclusion of women from this role is inconsistent with the fact that men and

women share equally in the life in Christ and therefore in his priesthood.

103 (c) All those opposed to the ordination of women point to passages in the Bible which teach that women are to be subordinate to men both in the world and in the Church. This subordination is traced to one of the two stories in Genesis of the creation and fall. It is reinforced by some of the practical teaching found in the Pauline corpus of letters, according to which women should not speak or teach in the Church. Those in favour of the ordination of women claim that woman's subordination to man was overcome in Christ (Gal. 3.28), and they point out that very few Churches now carry out to the letter all the practical teaching found in the Pauline letters. In most of our Churches, for instance, women have very important teaching roles, and are often admitted to the diaconate. The debate on this issue is closely tied to a particular interpretation of the authority of Scripture.

104 Whatever the outcome, we believe that this debate should be carried on in the context of the mission of the Christian Church to the whole of humanity. What kind of ministry in the Church will witness most faithfully and effectively to the fullness of Christ's ministry? What kind of ministry will enable the Church to convey to contemporary society the good news that in Christ God has reconciled the whole of humanity to himself? The debate is not simply about the ministry. It concerns the nature of the Church and of Christ's salvation of humanity, and is indeed central to our understanding of the nature and being of God.

V OUR GOAL

The Form of Unity

105   We are at one in believing that God intends the unity of his Church, but along with our partners in the ecumenical movement, we still struggle to understand and express the form which unity should take. It is clear that the Church – like the human family as a whole – is and will always be characterized by great diversity. People differ according to national and political allegiance, ethnic and cultural character, and the thought forms embodied in their various languages. These differences will always be present among Christians, both within denominations and between them. Because the Church is called to be a sign and the first-fruits of God's purpose to reconcile all things in Christ, its provisional character will only be truly expressed if these diversities are also present in its life, and are yet at the same time held within a unity which bears witness to God's final purpose. Its life must, if it is to be true to its nature, neither destroy this diversity by the imposition of a false and premature unity which pretends to embody what will only be truly known at the end; nor absolutize the diverse elements by allowing them to destroy the unity which is Christ's gift. To put the matter another way: the sovereign grace of God in Christ which holds us together must not be regarded as a wholly hidden reality which does not have to be expressed in visible unity; nor, on the other hand, must we allow our premature vision of the final unity to deny the possibility that other visions may contain elements of truth.

106   What visible form of unity will correspond to this

character of the Church as the provisional embodiment
of an eschatological unity? During the greater part of
the Church's history, when human society was less
mobile than it is now, the divisions of the Church were
mainly geographical. The separated communions occupied, as a general rule, distinct areas. In the last three
hundred years, however, and especially since the creation of new nations in America by the emigration of
peoples from many different areas of Europe, the
Church in each area has been characterized by a plural-
ity of confessional allegiances. And because a mobile
society necessitates large-scale organization, denominational structures have been developed to support and
unify the local congregation scattered throughout a
religiously plural society and to co-ordinate their activities. The 'denomination' as we know it is essentially a
product of the North American experience during the
past two hundred years, and has now become the domi-
nant form of the Church in most parts of the world. No
one can deny that denominational organizations have
enabled the churches to act effectively in many ways,
and it is difficult to imagine the Church today without
them. Yet, as theologians have pointed out, their
ecclesial status is very questionable. In the New Testament the word *ecclesia* is used to denote the local
fellowship, the church in a region (Acts 9.31) or the
universal Church. It is a questionable use of biblical
language to use the word 'church' for the entities which
we now call 'denominations'. Nevertheless there are
some who affirm that the form of visible unity to be
sought is the reconciliation of these denominations in
such a way as to enable them to continue to exist in
their present form while recognizing and accepting one
another as optional alternative manifestations of the one
holy catholic Church.

107   At its Third Assembly in New Delhi (1961), the WCC made the following statement about the form of visible unity:

> We believe that the unity which is both God's will and his gift to his Church is made visible as all in each place who are baptized into Jesus Christ and confess him as Lord and Saviour are brought by the Holy Spirit into one fully committed fellowship, holding the one apostolic faith, preaching the one Gospel, breaking the one bread, joining in common prayer, and having a corporate life reaching out in witness and service to all and who at the same time are united with the whole Christian fellowship in all places and all ages in such wise that ministry and members are accepted by all, and that all can act and speak together as occasion requires for the tasks to which God calls his people
>
> (New Delhi Report, p. 116)

108   At the Fourth Assembly in Uppsala (1968), this was further developed with special emphasis on its second part - namely the call to the 'churches in all places to realize that they belong together and are called to act together'. The Assembly went on:

> The ecumenical movement helps to enlarge this experience of universality, and its regional councils and its World Council may be regarded as a transitional opportunity for eventually actualizing a truly universal, ecumenical, conciliar form of common life and witness. The members of the World Council of Churches, committed to each other, should work for the time when a genuinely ecumenical council may once more speak for all Christians and lead the way into the future.
>
> (Uppsala Report, p. 17)

109   In later discussions this concept of 'conciliar fellowship' was further developed, not as an alternative to the model set forth at New Delhi but as the drawing out of one of its implications. The Fifth Assembly at Nairobi (1975) further clarified this concept in the following words:

The one Church is to be envisioned as a conciliar fellowship of local churches which are themselves truly united. In this conciliar fellowship, each local church possesses, in communion with the others, the fulness of catholicity, witnesses to the same apostolic faith, and therefore recognizes the others as belonging to the same Church of Christ and guided by the same Spirit.

(Nairobi Report, p. 60)

In the Vancouver Assembly (1983) the WCC re-committed itself to three things: (1) Visible unity, (2) Mission and evangelism, and (3) Justice and peace. It re-committed itself to visible unity in the following words:

The Lord prays for the unity of his people as a sign by which the world may be brought to faith, renewal and unity. We take slow, stumbling steps on the way to the visible unity of the Church, but we are sure the direction is essential to our faithfulness. Since the Nairobi Assembly there have been movements in many places, new united Churches, acts of common witness, local ecumenical projects. There is a new theological convergence which could enable decisive steps towards one eucharistic fellowship. We especially thank God for the hope given to us by the BEM document and seek widespread response to it.

(Vancouver Report, p. 2)

110 We believe that our two communions should endorse these ecumenical findings. This would imply that we are not simply seeking a *modus vivendi* between two globally organized denominations which would continue their separate though reconciled existence. Since we see the denomination not as by itself 'the Church', but as a family or fellowship of churches, we are agreed that Christian unity must in the last resort be discovered and actualized at the local level. Hence we seek the emergence of reconciled local communities, each of which is recognizable as 'church' in the proper

sense: i.e. communities which exhibit in each place the fullness of ministerial order, eucharistic fellowship, pastoral care, and missionary commitment and which, through mutual communion and co-operation, bear witness on the regional, national and even international levels. Such churches would express both the unity to which God calls his whole creation in Christ and the diversity which properly characterizes the human family as God intends it to be. While we can only speak as members of our two communions, our intention in speaking of 'locally recognizable forms of the universal Church' is obviously directed to all who are called by Christ's name. Our hope is that our member churches might play a part in drawing together others also into something which might express locally the wholeness of the catholic Church.

111   But what, exactly, is meant by the use of the word 'local' in this connection? This question raises complex issues. Anglican polity implies a diocesan structure based on the bishop, a Reformed, a pres-byterial or congregational one. In both traditions, however, popular understanding regards the local congregation meeting weekly for worship as the basic unit, and this should not be written off as a complete misunderstanding, since the fullness of the catholic Church is there in the eucharistic celebration of the Sunday assembly of the people of God. But if the Church is to be truly the sign and foretaste of God's Kingdom for the place where it is, we have to take into account not only our church traditions but the realities of the secular world in which the 'local' church must make its witness. Except in very simple static societies, modern communities consist of various over-lapping groups whose members are related through

language, work, culture and common interest. In order to be effective in missionary outreach the Church may have to encourage the formation of distinct forms of ministry and eucharistic fellowship for different groups in the same area. Yet these must be enabled to realize their unity through sharing the life of a diocese, presbytery or association. But even a large diocese, if it is small enough to have the real experience of unity, may be too small to embrace the life of a modern city. There is thus no simple definition of the phrase 'local church' which is applicable to all situations, but we commend the following statement by a recent WCC consultation on the subject:

> The term refers to an area where Christians can easily meet and form one committed fellowship in witness and service. Every local church will normally gather in one eucharistic service. The conditions of the area may be such that there is need of several separate services. Even then it must be made evident that these communities understand themselves as one eucharistic fellowship.
>
> The area to be served may vary in size. It may be a village or a small town; it may be a city or part of a city. It should not be so large that the Christian community loses coherence, nor yet so small that its homogeneity favours separatism in the human community. The area should be so chosen that the power of the Gospel to cross human barriers will be made manifest.
>
> ('In Each Place: Towards a Fellowship of Local Churches Truly United', WCC 1977, pp. 8-9)

Our differing structures, congregational and diocesan, have arisen in the course of seeking to be faithful to our calling to manifest the new life in Christ in and for each local community. As we seek together the proper forms of a locally united Church we cannot give exclusive importance either to the single congregation or to a larger diocese or presbytery. We must recognize the secular realities of each place, and seek forms of local unity and ministerial order which will manifest for each place the fullness of Christ's redeeming presence and power.

Practical Suggestions

112   If our two communions are to become one, Reformed churches will have to face the question of bishops, Anglican churches will have to reconsider the diaconate and take into account the Reformed experience of the eldership, and both communions will have to take more seriously the role of the whole membership in the governance of the Church. The following suggestions will not fit all the circumstances but are set out in order to stimulate study of workable structures which may be appropriate in each area.

(a) It is recognized in both communions that the Reformed pattern, in which each local congregation has a minister assisted by a body of elders is in conformity with a pattern which seems to have been common in the earliest times. The Reformed minister occupies a place analogous to that of the primitive bishops. In this sense the Reformed may rightly say: 'We have bishops already'.

(b) It is recognized that the concept of the 'local church' is different in the two traditions: for Anglicans it is the diocese centred in the bishop; for Reformed it is the congregation meeting weekly for the sharing of word and sacrament under the presidency of the minister. However we define the 'local church', we all believe that in every such gathering the full ministry of word and sacrament ought to be available as an integral part of the life of the congregation.

(c) Even though the Reformed might rightly say that they have bishops already, it is accepted in most Reformed churches that some form of oversight is needed at a supra-congregational level. Normally this oversight is exercised by a corporate body – presbytery or synod. We think that Reformed churches should accept the fact that, at every level, oversight needs to be exercised in a way that is both personal and corporate. Personal oversight apart from the wisdom of a corporate body is apt to become arbitrary and erratic; oversight by a corporate body without a personal pastor is apt to become bureaucratic and legalistic. In fact many Reformed churches have developed forms of oversight at the regional level which combine both elements effectively.

(d) It is agreed by all that personal oversight is to be exercised by participation in the one Good Shepherd; if not it is corrupted and corrupting.

113   What changes would be involved in Reformed practice if the moderator of presbytery or synod were to become a bishop-in-presbytery? We think that the following would be involved:

(a) He would have to hold office for a substantial period, sufficient to enable him to develop a real pastoral relationship with ministers and people and to be known widely in the community as the representative of the Church in the particular area.

(b) The bishop would have to be relieved of other duties in order to fulfil this role.

(*c*) The bishop's role would be more than that of presiding at meetings. The following extract from the ordination prayer for a bishop from the Church of England's Alternative Service Book may indicate the most important elements in the work of a bishop:

> Almighty Father, fill this your servant with the grace and power which you gave to your apostles, that he may lead those committed to his charge in proclaiming the gospel of salvation. Through him increase your Church, renew its ministry and unite its members in a holy fellowship of truth and love. Enable him as a true shepherd to feed and govern your flock; make him wise as a teacher, and steadfast as a guardian of its faith and sacraments. Guide and direct him in presiding at the worship of your people. Give him humility, that he may use his authority to heal, not to hurt; to build up, not to destroy.

In other words, the one so ordained would be called to ministerial leadership in the whole life of the Church in his area.

(*d*) The bishop would need to have opportunities to share with his colleagues in other presbyteries in order to seek help and wisdom in dealing with pastoral problems. It is a matter for discussion whether this should take the form of a 'college of bishops' exercising a distinct role in the constitutional government of the Church, as in Anglican practice; or whether it should take the form of provision for regular consultation on pastoral problems without such a separate governing role as in the CSI.

114 Such a suggestion may not commend itself initially to some Reformed ministers. We would, how-

ever, commend it on the following grounds: that in every walk of life there ought to be a visible element of personal accountability; that every minister, including the bishop, needs personal pastoral support and help in his ministry; and that in his exercise of personal oversight the moderator/bishop would really be acting pastorally.

115   We also anticipate that the suggestions may meet with resistance from presbyteries on the ground that something of their present authority would be diminished. We believe, on the contrary, that an effective and sustained personal leadership, if rightly exercised, is the best way to ensure the authority and effectiveness of a corporate body such as a synod or presbytery.

116   In many languages there are several words which are used or may be appropriately used for the office of chief pastor. Each word has its distinctive overtones of meaning. It is not necessary that the same word should always be used, provided that the substance of the office is recognizably the same. There have been and are great variations in the ways in which the episcopal office is exercised, and while Reformed churches ought not necessarily to copy any existing Anglican model, there ought to be discussion among the churches with a view to developing styles of oversight which are congruous with the biblical witness and the practice of the universal Church, and which are appropriate to contemporary circumstances.

117   If the two traditions are to come together in united churches, Anglicans will have to consider both the meaning and practice of the diaconate and also the significance of the eldership as it has been developed in the Reformed tradition. Anglicans are aware of the fact

that the diaconate as at present exercised in many of their churches is not a genuine diaconate in any classical or biblical sense, but is rather a period of probation and preparation for the priesthood. Many Anglicans have been much concerned for a long time to seek the restoration of a genuine diaconate, and there are parts of the communion where this is taking place. In the eldership God has raised up collegial ministry which has clear mandate in the New Testament and which has proved effective in the contemporary world in many different situations. We think that Anglicans should adopt the eldership as it has developed in the Reformed tradition in order to give shape to emerging movements of lay leadership in the Anglican Churches. This would mean the development of a number of elders in every congregation, normally non-stipendiary and not intending to serve later as priests, sharing with the priest in the pastoral care of the congregation in a manner which might follow in large measure the pattern offered by the present Reformed eldership. It is recognized, of course, that the words 'deacon' and 'elder' in the early Church stand for quite distinct offices. But it is also recognized (e.g. in BEM, p. 24, para. 22) that 'the Spirit has many times led the Church to adapt its ministry to contextual needs', and that the present function of the deacon in the Anglican church is pastoral rather than 'diaconal' in the classical sense. There is therefore no reason why the experience of the Reformed eldership should not be made use of to enrich a renewed Anglican diaconate.

118   If such an office of elder/deacon is to be accepted for all congregations in future united churches, it would be essential to ensure that the entire membership of the congregation is enabled to take its proper share in the

governance of the Church. This would require provision for regular meetings of the whole congregation to consider matters affecting the life and witness of the Church, and regular opportunities for the entire membership to choose representatives to act on its behalf in the governance of the congregation and of the wider Church. The question whether such representatives should or should not necessarily be elders/deacons is one which would have to be discussed. We cite here the model of the Congregation in the Uniting Church of Australia:

> The Congregation is the embodiment in one place of the One Holy Catholic and Apostolic Church, worshipping, witnessing and serving as a fellowship of the Spirit in Christ. Its members meet regularly to hear God's Word, to celebrate the sacraments, to build one another up in love, to share in the wider responsibilities of the Church, and to serve the world. The congregation will recognise the need for a diversity of agencies for the better ordering of her life in such matters as education, administration and finance.
>
> (Basis of Union)

119   Nothing said in this report should be taken to imply that ordained ministry is all we need. In concentrating attention on the steps required towards unity, we take it for granted that the life of the churches will be sustained as in any period of Christian history, by a great variety of lay ministries, full-time, part-time and voluntary – ministries raised up to meet needs, giving effective service and not to be regretted when their time passes.

Expectations of the Present Report.

120   In offering this Report to our parent bodies, we

recognize that our member churches are in many vastly different cultural and political situations. We hope that the Report will, so far as possible, be studied by Anglican and Reformed congregations together in each place. We hope that the guidelines we have suggested will be useful to Anglican and Reformed churches in different parts of the world who are seeking unity. We are encouraged by the degree of convergence already visible as each of our two communions seeks to reform itself. For example, the Reformed welcome the Anglican trend towards ministering baptism in the Sunday assembly of the people of God, and Anglicans welcome the trend towards more frequent celebration of the Eucharist in Reformed churches.

121 The movement for unity has suffered in recent years because bilateral international discussions between confessional families have dealt mainly with theological questions, while the many multilateral discussions between churches in each place (e.g. in local councils of churches) have dealt mainly with practical issues, and the two have not been brought together. We hope that the theological work done in this Report will be studied in relation to the practical problems in each place, and that, if possible, it will be studied by groups representing more than our two communions. In such local discussions the work of these bilateral theological discussions, and the WCC document on *Baptism, Eucharist and Ministry* should be made use of. In order to facilitate discussion and promote the consideration of possible action, we have appended a number of questions to the Report. We would welcome responses to these questions not only from our member churches but also from any national or local councils of churches which see fit to study our work.

122   We are aware of the fact that the things which keep Anglicans and Reformed in any particular place apart are often not the things dealt with in 'Faith and Order' documents. The divisive factors are often of other kinds – cultural, social and political. We have to ask whether the widespread failure of our member churches to act on the convictions which they hold in common is not the result of lethargy, of timidity, or unwillingness to face change and, above all, of an acquiescence in social injustice and a lack of missionary zeal. In the present report we have repeatedly stressed the fact that it is in a missionary context that the true nature of the Church, sacraments and ministry are understood. We cannot receive our proper unity without this missionary context. It is because we have been grasped by the vision of the Kingdom of God that we are motivated to overcome divisions. As the churches in each place study this report together, they should ask one another whether this missionary perspective is in fact controlling their study.

123   We hope that those who study this Report will have in mind seven things which we have tried to keep in view:

(*a*) Participation in Christ and in the life of the triune God. In our different communions we are all participating, in the Spirit, in what Christ has done and is doing, and in his communion with the Father and his mission to the world and his will for peace and justice.

(*b*) The primacy of grace. We are in Christ simply by the sheer unconditioned grace of our Lord who has taken us, unworthy as we are, into his company. We do not seek unity because we can approve of one another. We seek it because, when we refuse to do so, we treat with contempt the immeasurable kindness of our Lord who has accepted us as we are in order that he may make us what he would have us to be.

(c) The world is torn apart and threatened with destruction by our selfish passion, greed and fear. The Church cannot be the sign of God's reconciling grace for all humankind while itself remaining unreconciled, stubbornly clinging to the past.

(d) The missionary calling. The Church is the first-fruits of God's gracious purpose to embrace his whole human family in the arms of his love. While we think only of ourselves and of what is helpful to us, we miss what he has in store for us. It is when we turn towards the world as witnesses, heralds and servants of his Kingdom, that we shall learn the secret of unity.

(e) The other discussions – bilateral and multilateral – in which our two communions have taken part (see Appendix 1).

(f) The experience of united churches. Our two traditions are represented (with others) in the united churches of the Indian sub-continent, the formation of which was inspired by the vision of a church locally united and reflecting in its local unity the unity of the universal Church. These churches have now a long and precious experience of living and growing together in unity. Those who laboured and prayed for the union of these churches believed that their example would encourage others to follow, but this hope has been disappointed. The united churches, instead of being the vanguard of a movement for unity, have become isolated. In contradiction of their own purpose, they are in danger of being seen as just a new denomination. We think it imperative that, as far as possible, they should be drawn into the further discussions with us, both so that their experience may be available to us, and also that their threatened isolation may be avoided. We would hope that other world confessional families which are involved in the Indian unions (Methodists, Baptists, Disciples, Lutherans) would wish to take similar actions in so far as they are involved in bi-lateral conversations.

(g) The experience for many of our member churches who have received mutual encouragement and correction through their membership in the World Council of Churches.

124   Throughout our conversations we have been led to see all our work in the perspective of the Church's missionary calling, acknowledging that the Church is but a provisional embodiment of what is promised at the end. The Church is – to use again the familiar image – a pilgrim people. The Church must therefore be willing to move when the Lord calls it to do so. This is our final, and perhaps most important word. Many of the gravest warnings in Scripture are addressed to those who are unwilling to move forward in response to the call and promise of God (e.g. Heb. 3.12-19). The call to unity challenges our sloth and unbelief with a summons to look up and listen to the voice of the living God who has called us to be one as he is one, and who is able to complete what he has begun in us. We may well take to ourselves the call addressed to an unbelieving company on the brink of the Red Sea: 'Tell the people of Israel to go forward' (Exod. 14.15).

VI RECOMMENDATIONS

1 We invite Anglican and Reformed Churches to pray for each other regularly. To this end we ask the Anglican Consultative Council and the World Alliance of Reformed Churches to find ways of encouraging the widest possible use of the Ecumenical Prayer Cycle, and we ask the Anglican Consultative Council to relate the Anglican Prayer Cycle more closely to the Ecumenical Prayer Cycle.

2 Having regard to the differing degrees of relationship between the churches of our two communions in various parts of the world, we urge them to embark on the next stage towards unity, in the light of the findings of this report.

3 We recommend that our member Churches examine carefully the issues raised under the heading 'What keeps us apart' (paras. 6–14).

4 We recommend that the churches of both traditions undertake a fresh examination of the implications of our common practice of baptism – wherever possible together, but certainly sharing their findings.

5 We recommend that where churches of our two communions are committed to going forward to seek visible unity, a measure of *reciprocal* communion should be made possible; for communion is not only a sign of unity achieved, but also a means by which God brings it about.

6 We recommend that the churches of our two communions examine their structures to see if the personal, collegial and communal aspects of oversight are adequately represented at every level; and that if they are not, they give serious attention to such revisions as are applicable in their regions.

7 We recommend that our member Churches in each place explore the possibility of moving towards the formation of united churches as envisaged in section V in this report.

8 In the light of what we have said in paragraphs 22, 44, 45, 61 and 70 of this report we recommend that, wherever possible, Anglican and Reformed Churches seek together ways in which all forms of discrimination which devalue persons may be eliminated. As a step in this direction we urge our churches around the world:

(*a*) to work together to overcome those barriers which exist between privileged and underprivileged, black and white, male and female;

(*b*) to share their human, spiritual and material resources with those in need.

9 We recommend that our churches discuss the following questions at all levels – in joint groups where possible:

General Questions

1 God has accepted us and made us one in Christ. Therefore we are bound to accept one another and live together in one body. How must we change in order to enable us to be one body in each place? (paras. 19ff.)

2   Are the concerns for evangelism, social justice and doc-
    trinal purity compatible with the active struggle for unity?
    How in your experience are they held together? (paras.
    29ff.)

3   Does your church engage in mission? Why is mission impor-
    tant? Are the motives for mission the same as, or different
    from, the motives for unity? (paras. 35ff.)

4   Are the obstacles listed in Section I a sufficient ground for
    our remaining separate? (paras. 6ff.)

5   What form and extent of doctrinal agreement is necessary
    for the reunion of separate Christian churches? What relation
    does your answer have to the measure of agreement within
    your own church?

6   How far is folk religion a barrier to unity?

7   For good and for ill, in what ways is your church bound to
    and moulded by your culture, or by an alien culture?

8   How is your church conditioned by a sense of national
    identity?

9   In what ways is your church related to the state?

10 What are the implications of your answers to questions 7, 8
    and 9 for your understanding of:
       (i) the nature of the Church;
      (ii) the Lordship of Christ in his Church;
     (iii) the prophetic role of the Church *vis à vis* the State;
      (iv) the mission of the Church?

11 What importance has historic continuity in the Church for
    the life of the ordinary Christian? How is this continuity
    maintained? (Section IV)

12 What difference does the consciousness of belonging to a
    universal Church make to the ordering of your church life
    and mission? (Section V)

Questions relating to worship and the sacraments

1   What is the significance of people feeling uncomfortable
    in each other's worship for relations between the churches?

Should sharing in each other's worship enrich us, or give us reasons for remaining apart?

2　To what extent do stereotyped images of other people's practices and institutions constitute a barrier to reunion, and what can be done to correct these?

3　Since baptism, as the rite of Christian initiation, is sufficient to constitute a person a full member of Christ and his Church, what is the theological and pastoral purpose of confirmation or any analogous rite, and how are both related to participation in the Eucharist? (paras. 55ff., 72)

4　The report states that Christ constitutes his Church in the Eucharist. What are the implications of this for the regularity and frequency of communion? (paras. 62ff.)

5　For participation in the Eucharist it is required that we be in love and charity with our neighbours. We are in fact involved in structures of violence and oppression. What steps are you taking to deal with this contradiction?

6　Is the statement about 'lay celebration' of the Lord's Supper (para. 83) acceptable? If not, why not?

7　What does your church do with the consecrated elements left over after communion? What does this imply concerning your understanding of Christ's presence?

Questions on ministry and church membership

1　Since both our communions recognize each other's baptism, what prevents us from establishing full communion, accepting each other's members and mutually exchanging ministers as vital steps on the road to full unity?

2　To what extent does the kind of ministry exercised by your ordained ministers encourage or inhibit the ministry of the whole body?

3　Of the names you normally use for the ordained minister which do you think most appropriate to the task of the ministry of word and sacrament and of Christian leadership? What is the value in the names you do not normally use? (para. 79)

4   In any plan of union in your area how could the conti-
     nuity of ordination with the undivided Church be restored,
     whilst the reality of God's gift of ministry to all participat-
     ing churches is acknowledged?

5   Is the description of ordination given in paras. 80-90
     acceptable to both our communions?

6   To what extent is the ministry of your church at every level
     effectively personal, collegial and communal?

7   What changes would be needed in your area for Reformed
     churches to adopt a 'bishop-in-presbytery' and for Anglican
     churches to accept the office of elder, as suggested in
     paras. 112-16?

8   What patterns of ministry would be appropriate for a
     united church in your area, given the missionary task of the
     Church, the existing patterns in both communions, and the
     need for ministries to be acceptable to both world com-
     munions?

9   How should the ordained and non-ordained ministries at all
     levels be ordered so that ministers are always mutually
     accountable and responsible?

10   Does the practice of your church bear witness to the equal
     partnership of women and men in God's covenant? How
     could your church incorporate women more fully into
     every facet of its ministry and governance? (paras. 98-104)

11   There are some who believe that it is God's will to ordain
     women to the ministry, and others who do not. There will
     not be full unity between our two communions until we
     reach a common mind on this issue. What steps are our
     churches in your area taking together to seek God's will on
     this matter? Are women represented in all your discussions
     of this issue?

12   In the discussion of the ordination of women, what weight
     ought to be given to the effects of our decisions on other
     churches?

APPENDIX 1

Reports of principal bilateral and multilateral
conversations in which Anglicans and Reformed
have recently been engaged

Baptism, Eucharist and Ministry. Faith and Order Paper no. 111.
World Council of Churches, Geneva 1982.

The Final Report. Anglican–Roman Catholic International
Commission (ARCIC). Windsor, 1981. CTS/SPCK, London
1982.

Anglican-Orthodox Dialogue. The Moscow Agreed Statement.
Anglican-Orthodox Joint Doctrinal Commission 1976. SPCK,
London 1977.

Anglican–Lutheran International Conversations. The Report of
the Conversations 1970–1972 authorized by the Lambeth
Conference and the Lutheran World Federation: Pullach,
1972. SPCK, London 1973.

Lutheran–Episcopal Dialogue. The Report of the Lutheran–
Episcopal Dialogue: Second Series 1976–1980. Forward
Movement Publications, Cincinnati 1981.

The Presence of Christ in the Church and the World (Reformed–
Roman Catholic). World Alliance of Reformed Churches/
Secretariat for Promoting Christian Unity 1977.

The Leuenberg Agreement (Lutheran–Reformed). *Ecumenical
Review* XXV no. 3, July 1973.

Report of Theological Conversations (Baptist–Reformed). World
Alliance of Reformed Churches/Baptist World Alliance 1977.

APPENDIX 2

List of Participants

REFORMED

The Revd John Huxtable (co-chairman to 1982)
Formerly General Secretary, United Reformed Church, UK

The Revd Roy F. Wilson (co-chairman from 1983)
Minister, United Church of Canada

The Revd Dr Christian Baeta
Formerly Professor for the Study of Religions, University of Ghana

The Revd Gordon Grant
Board of World Mission and Unity, Church of Scotland

The Revd Stuart Louden
Minister Emeritus, Greyfriars, Edinburgh

The Rt Revd Lesslie Newbigin
Minister, Winson Green United Reformed Church. Birmingham, England

The Revd Edwin Pons (1981)
United Church of Zambia

The Revd Robert Samson (from 1982)
Deputy General Secretary, Presbyterian Church of Southern Africa

The Revd George Yule
Professor of Church History, University of Aberdeen, Scotland

The Revd Dr Lukas Vischer (1983 only)
Director, Swiss Protestant Office for Ecumenism

The Revd James Torrance (consultant, 1983–4)
Professor of Systematic Theology, University of Aberdeen, Scotland

The Revd Richmond Smith (co-secretary, 1981–3)
Secretary, Department of Theology, World Alliance of Reformed Churches

The Revd Alan Sell (co-secretary, 1984)
Secretary, Department of Theology, World Alliance of Reformed Churches

ANGLICAN

The Rt Revd John Tinsley (co-chairman)
Bishop of Bristol

The Rt Revd Sigqibo Dwane
Bishop of the Order of Ethiopia, Church of the Province of Southern Africa

Canon Robert Halliday
Rector, St Andrew's Episcopal Church, St Andrew's, Scotland

The Revd Andrew Kirk
Associate Director, London Institute for Contemporary Christianity, and Theologian Missioner, Church Missionary Society

The Revd Richard A. Norris Jr
Professor of Church History, Union Theological Seminary, New York

The Revd John Nyesi
Department of Rural Development, Diocese of Maseno South, Kenya

Canon Martin Reardon
Secretary, Board for Mission and Unity, Church of England

The Revd Louis Weil (consultant, 1983–4)
Professor of Liturgics, Nashotah House, Wisconsin, USA

The Revd George Braund (co-secretary)
Ecumenical Secretary, Anglican Consultative Council

WORLD COUNCIL OF CHURCHES

The Revd Michael Kinnamon (1981)
Executive Secretary, Faith and Order

APPENDIX 3

Papers contributed to the Commission

1978 - PREPARATORY MEETING

Yule: Church Union Negotiations - Australia and New Zealand.

Baeta: Church Union Negotiations, Ghana, 1978.

Norris: The Consultation on Church Union.

Louden: Analysis of specific Anglican and Reformed Theological questions which require further examination.

Dwane: A Third World Contribution to the Anglican-Reformed Theological Consultation.

Reardon: Analysis of the specific Anglican and Reformed Theological questions from an Anglican point of view.

1981

Yule: Incarnation and the Unity of the Church.

Kirk: The Kingdom, the Messiah and the Church's witness in Latin America.

Newbigin: Kingdom and Church: a reflection on the papers of Yule and Kirk.

1982

Norris: What is 'Church Unity'?

Dwane: To what extent should orthopraxis be either a condition of, means to, or result of Church Unity?

Huxtable: What is the content, context and goal of the Church's Mission?

1983

Grant and Halliday: Memorandum on agreed positions and further issues.

Huxtable and Dwane: Theological correspondence on the issue of Word, Sacraments and Ministry.

Newbigin: How should we understand Sacraments and Ministry?